STUDIES IN FRENCH LITERATURE No. 25

General Editor
W. G. Moore
Emeritus Fellow of St John's College, Oxford

To Frederick and Martha Hallett

PROUST:
DU CÔTÉ DE
CHEZ SWANN

by
VALERIE MINOGUE

Lecturer in French, Queen Mary College, University of London

EDWARD ARNOLD

© VALERIE MINOGUE 1973

First published 1973
by Edward Arnold (Publishers) Ltd
25 Hill Street, London W1X 8LL

Cloth edition ISBN: 0 7131 5720 8
Paper edition ISBN: 0 7131 5721 6

Printed in Great Britain by
The Camelot Press Ltd, London and Southampton

Contents

Acknowledgements

The publishers wish to thank Editions Gallimard, Paris, for permission to print copyright material from *Du Côté de chez Swann*, by Marcel Proust, edited by Pierre Clarac and André Ferré (1968).

1. Introduction

The name Marcel Proust, like the kaleidoscope to which he so often refers, offers a great variety of different images. There is Proust the fashionable man-about-town, and Proust the asthmatic, the homosexual and neurotic; there is a Jewish Proust, passionate in the defence of the innocent Dreyfus, and a Catholic Proust, steeped in the culture and symbolism of the Church; there is Proust the cynic, Proust the idealist, Proust the mimic and wit. There is even a positivist, drawing up the fundamental laws of human conduct. And we should add perhaps the caricatural Proust of the cultural comic-strip—the ailing but indefatigable creator of a work whose length and complexity make the average novel look as insubstantial as the back of a cornflakes packet.

In a study of such limited scope, it is impossible to do justice to all these varying aspects. I have therefore concentrated my attention on the emergence in *Du Côté de chez Swann* of what Marcel calls 'la vocation invisible dont cet ouvrage est l'histoire' (II, 397).[1] He means the vocation to art, of which Marcel has intermittent intimations, and which at last he joyfully embraces. As an artist, Proust seeks to create one of those works in which 'il n'y a pas une seule touche qui soit isolée, où chaque partie reçoit des autres sa raison d'être comme elle leur impose la sienne' (II, 537). No note is separate; each part is closely linked with every other part, to create a rich and resonant orchestration of manifold themes. The characters, the ideas and the themes of this first volume recur in changing patterns throughout the whole novel. Proust once said he conceived of the novel as one continuous sentence. That 'sentence' expresses his own experience of life, in a form that contains the essence of that 'vraie vie' for which he was always searching.

And what is the 'vraie vie'? It is life distilled in the innermost recesses of individual consciousness. Truth, Marcel learns conclusively at the end of the novel, is not in the surface or the single facts and events of life. It can only be represented in flux and movement. It is not a matter of

[1] Page references to *A la Recherche du Temps perdu* give the volume and page numbers in the 1968 *Pléiade* edition, edited by Pierre Clarac and André Ferré.

capturing isolated 'privileged moments', but a matter of learning from certain complex moments of experience that past and present are indissolubly united, and that beneath the vagaries and vicissitudes of life, there subsists, stubbornly, a unique, endlessly variable, yet recognizable self. Proust's novel is the pursuit of the truth of that self, and the recomposition of the otherwise inaccessible reality of the inner world.

Du Côté de chez Swann is thus the first part of a very complex novel. And Proust does not make it easy for the reader by stating at the outset who and what his characters are, nor does he offer a straightforward chronological progression. His unusual treatment of chronology is no gratuitous contrivance, for it is vital that the reader be inducted into a complex temporal world where past and present fuse. We must see Marcel's life as it seemed to him at different points of the past, and as it seems now to Marcel the mature narrator—and occasionally, as it has seemed at various points between the 'then' of experience, and the 'now' of narration. For time, in its movement, changes the narrator and his view of his past. It transforms the apparently sterile Marcel into a creator, capable of translating his life into a work of art that uniquely celebrates the beauty, poetry and joy of being alive.

2. 'Du Côté de chez Swann': The Creation of a Personal Language

La vraie vie . . . c'est la littérature . . . le style pour l'écrivain aussi bien que la couleur pour le peintre, est une question non de technique mais de vision. Il est la révélation, qui serait impossible par les moyens directs et conscients, de la différence qualitative dans la façon dont nous apparaît le monde, différence qui, s'il n'y avait pas l'art, resterait le secret éternel de chacun. Par l'art seulement nous pouvons sortir de nous, savoir ce que voit un autre de cet univers qui n'est pas le même que le nôtre. (III, 895)

What Proust is concerned to express lies beyond the common currency of language. We are to see the world of human experience with other eyes, criss-crossed by the patterns of other memories and associations. We are to enter into the vision of another and, through art, participate in the unique quality of his experience.

Such participation is rare in human communication. We may take pride in the irreducible individuality of each human being, but we are also trapped within that individuality. The language we use when we try to go beyond the surface of our experience has roots in sensation and memory, and these roots require lengthy explanation if we are really to share the quick of our experience. Indeed, our most vivid sensations and profound perceptions often defy communication, and we are reduced to inarticulate exclamations which convey only our excitement—like Marcel on that autumn day in Combray when he shouts excitedly 'Zut, zut, zut, zut!' (I, 155). Proust creates for us a new language which will make articulate what previously was inarticulate, and communicate what was locked up in the privacy of the individual. *Du Côté de chez Swann* is an introduction to this personal language. It uncovers for us the roots of Marcel's vocabulary and syntax, the fundamental and recurring patterns that have formed his style.

It is by laying bare the process by which Marcel's personal language is formed that Proust tries to get beyond the ordinary barriers of communication and allow us to enter fully into the quality of Marcel's experience. The very words and names which Marcel uses (*Guermantes*, *lilas, aubépines, l'église*, for instance) acquire not merely the communicative power which words have in ordinary language, but also the rich connotative power which words have in the intimacy of inner experience. We learn not only what corresponds with the words in ordinary reality, but the other shadowy sides of words—the memories, expectations or sensations attached to them. The word *aubépine* is not merely a botanical description. It is a focus for memories of walks in Combray, of Tansonville and Gilberte, and of the church in Combray. It brings together things as diverse as the taste of cream-cheese mixed with strawberries and the freckles of Mlle Vinteuil. Later in the novel, the experience of the hawthorns teaches Marcel how to look at the sea in Balbec. The word *aubépine* thus becomes a living word in an organic 'vocabulary' which is unique to Marcel, yet accessible to the reader. Through the richness of this 'vocabulary' we are offered not merely the means—which ordinary language offers—to identify what we know and can recognize, but the means to explore the very quick of another's experience of life. The name 'Swann', similarly, is not a mere label, identifying once and for all a clearly-outlined figure. It indicates the stranger whose visits bring anguish to the child Marcel, and also the worldly man-about-town whose social prestige is so ill-recognized by the family at Combray. It achieves a new dimension in the relation of Swann's love for Odette, and later in the novel acquires new depths and meanings as we see Swann in new lights and new situations. The connotations of the name change for Marcel and the reader. At the same time Swann's life and experiences become specific terms which allow a better grasp of the patterns and movements of Marcel's own life. Swann's experiences become, as it were, the concepts of Marcel's understanding of his own life.

We learn to see through the eyes of Marcel. But this common metaphor may be misleading, for we do not learn to see through a pair of stable lenses, but through living—and consequently changing—eyes. In gaining access to Marcel's personal language, we gain access to a language constantly evolving in response to the shifts and changes of the world in time. Language, in Proust's use of it, is not just a way of expressing a vision, but is the ever-changing vision itself. Conventional language is apt to immobilize, to encase what was living and changing in fixed and rigid structures. Proust attempts by the vivacity and mobility of his language and style to counteract these hardening effects and render the living and changing in living and changing structures.

Marcel's vision, like Marcel's language, is subjective and exploratory:

it breaks down conventional categorizations. Most of the fixed points to which we are accustomed in literature—the permanence of human character, the stability of human emotions, the accuracy of the narrator's observation—are dissolved. The conventional notion of character is shown, in Marcel's vision, as no more than an *ad hoc* abstraction. The ordinary concept of emotion—love, for instance—is discarded, for it is seen as no more than a convenient piece of terminology covering the most discontinuous and disparate movements of the mind and heart. The narrator's observation is never total and never definitive: it is never better than partial, in both senses of the word. Paradoxically, so resolute and self-conscious a subjectivity can only be created by a mind capable of regarding its own passions and prejudices with objectivity and detachment. Truth itself, in Marcel's vision, whether it be social, psychological or political, seems merely evanescent, and the seizing of it is less a triumph than a self-flattering illusion. Beauty, whether in nature or in art, is an uncertain quantity. Is Mme de Guermantes a beautiful and noble creature bathed in the colours of history, or a red-faced woman with a big nose? Is Odette a faded *cocette*, or an embodiment of the loveliness of Botticelli's Zéphora? Is Bergotte's style a repository of unfailing beauty, or merely of 'des subtilités de mandarin déliquescent' (I, 474)? Proust does not even fall back on that common artistic shibboleth—the immortality of art. He reminds us that the human world is ultimately doomed to extinction and that 'La durée éternelle n'est pas plus promise aux œuvres qu'aux hommes' (III, 1043).

The only fixed point in the novel is the consciousness of Marcel—a Marcel who is never definitive, for beyond Marcel the protagonist (already a complex and changing figure) is Marcel the narrator, who is always situated 'elsewhere', in no specific time or place. It is significant that we never catch a glimpse of Marcel actually sitting at a desk in a house penning the words we are reading. In the narrative, he is merely a potential writer. It is only at the end of *A la Recherche du Temps perdu* that he arrives at the understanding which precedes creation. Yet beyond the uncertain and ever-changing protagonist-narrator, we perceive the central consciousness of Marcel the creator, who has found unity and coherence in what seems to the protagonist merely confusion and change. The novel becomes, as it were, that central yet elusive consciousness: the novel *is* his vision. Moments and moods cohere, and, again paradoxically, out of the contingent and ephemeral Proust creates an enduring monument. The reader is left convinced, at the end of the novel, of the reality and value of individual life, for the novel presents both the conviction and the proof that the identity of the self is a real value, capable of being rescued from time's destructive hands, and capable, through art, of a communication that transcends man's desperate solitude.

Three beginnings

Proust takes the reader into the intimacy of Marcel's world by a very artfully-planned route, for we must not be allowed to imagine that that world is a fixed point in space and time. We shall be forced 'by indirections' to 'find directions out'.

Du Côté de chez Swann is divided into three parts, *Combray, Un Amour de Swann* and *Noms de Pays: le Nom*.[1] *Combray* introduces us to Marcel's childhood and his family in the countryside of Combray. *Un Amour de Swann*, as though to ensure that we take no point of time as a definitive starting-point, takes us back to 'un amour que Swann avait eu avant ma naissance'. The third part, *Noms de Pays: le Nom*, explores the meanings of names for Marcel, the particular emotions and images which they contain, and begins a parallelism between Swann and Marcel which is to grow in the course of the novel. The three parts are united by their all being slides from the kaleidoscope of Marcel's memory, and we are introduced to this notion in the earliest pages of the novel, where the mature narrator recalls the various rooms in which he has lain awake or dreamed as child, youth and man.

Combray itself may also be divided into three parts. We begin with the narrator's evocation of remembered rooms—a sequence which introduces the preoccupation with time that lies at the core of the novel. Are memories of our past life merely these insubstantial flitting forms, or can they be recaptured fully? More important, can we recapture the different selves we were when we experienced them? The question Proust implicitly suggests here is this: Can the artist, by some supreme feat of concentration, will, intuition and intelligence, capture the quintessence of his many selves as they have existed in the ever-changing epochs and

[1] This first volume, in Proust's original scheme, included two-thirds of the next volume, *A L'Ombre des Jeunes Filles en Fleurs*. The present place of *Noms de Pays: le Nom* as the third part of the first volume is due to Proust's later rearrangement of the text. For discussion of this point, see Maurice Bardèche, *Marcel Proust, romancier* (Paris, Les Sept Couleurs, 1971), pp. 301ff.

situations of his life? This is to state in general terms the challenge Proust takes up, and his novel may be seen as the triumphant response to that challenge.

Among the many rooms the narrator recalls in the first pages of *Combray* is the bedroom he slept in as a child. To reinforce the instability of the succession of memories, we see that bedroom not delineated in stable colours and contours but lit by the flickering light of a magic lantern. It is after this first restless sequence—a sequence of successive rooms, then of successive frames of the magic lantern—that we meet, in the second section of *Combray*, the 'pan lumineux'—the one part of Marcel's early life that is readily accessible to his conscious memory. This section centres on a bed-time drama, and the moment when Marcel, as a child, waited up disobediently for his mother's goodnight kiss, and by this apparently trivial act irretrievably marked his life with a sense of guilt and failure.

The famous incident of the *madeleine* follows this 'panel' of conscious memory. The middle-aged narrator, who remembered of Combray only the area surrounding the bed-time drama, tells how he comes in from a walk one day in Paris, and is given some tea and cake. The taste of the tea awakes in him long-forgotten areas of experience, for it recalls the 'tisane' offered him as a child by his aunt Léonie at Combray. This specific sensation stimulates an involuntary memory quite beyond the reach of his conscious recall, and restores to him a world otherwise inaccessible. Combray, no longer arranged by an intelligence that selects only what is relevant to a single structure of emotions, emerges rich and unbidden from the depths of a cup of linden tea. This newly-recaptured childhood world forms the substance of the third and principal section of *Combray*, in which the most fleeting moments of his early life are restored to the narrator's consciousness.

In the course of *Combray*, we learn a great deal of the 'vocabulary' of the child Marcel, we learn some of the landmarks of his life and mind, some of the fundamental patterns of his sensibility. Even the tiny sketches that show Marcel's first encounter with Gilberte in the park at Tansonville, and with Mme de Guermantes in the church at Combray, offer suggestive outlines of Marcel's later experience of love. His relationship with his mother offers a prophetic pattern of craving for affection, dependence, insecurity, and jealousy. Proust's art gives us both an analytical appreciation of the various elements composing Marcel's experience, and a powerful sense of the wholeness and uniqueness of that experience as it is lived. It reveals that the world is not what it at first seems to the child, and we learn this not as a commonplace of childhood experience but in quite specific terms: the snobbery of Legrandin, the cruelty of Françoise, the lesbianism of Mlle Vinteuil. We learn not merely the existence of such undesirable features, but the manner in which they each uniquely enter the life of the child, and there become the sounding-boards off which later experience will bounce with new resonance. We see the child recognizing the existence of certain dark areas within himself, and watch him in the process of making those 'lâches calculs' by which he moves from the exacting and intolerant sensitivity of childhood idealism to the sophisticated compromises of maturity and self-knowledge.

At the end of Combray, we return to an indefinite 'aujourd'hui', enriched by memories of childhood and haunted by the scent of lilac. The solid provincial contours dissolve in the morning light as the narrator is restored to a present in which Combray is, after all, only a part of the past. The resurrection of Combray was but one shake of the kaleidoscope, one slide of the magic lantern, one among the narrator's waking evocations of diverse places and times. We must start again.

In Un Amour de Swann we move from first-person narration to the new perspective offered by the third-person. We see Swann as the hero of a story from which Marcel, except in his vital role as narrator, is absent.[2] Yet Swann's story follows in the sequence of Marcel's evocations, and we have already learned, in Combray, of a certain affinity between Marcel and Swann, when we are told that Swann, better than anyone, would have understood Marcel's bed-time anguish. The story of Swann is indeed an important part of that geological formation of memories, whose striations and colours reveal, as Marcel tells us at the end of Combray, 'des différences d'origine, d'âge, de "formation"' (I, 186). Certain profound resemblances in the central preoccupations of Marcel and Swann make of Swann, as we read, a phantom Marcel, a Marcel-who-might-have-been. The narrator tells not just a story he knows, but one so deeply imprinted on his mind that it has become part of his own life. It is a vital part of the history of Marcel's language, and it is a parable.

Rather than offering us the chronological development of Marcel the

[2] But the narrator's viewpoint is often merged with the subjectivity of Swann: see B. G. Rogers, Proust's Narrative Techniques (Geneva, Droz, 1965), pp. 123–6.

child, followed by Marcel the adolescent, Proust interpolates the relation of an adult drama, which clarifies and intensifies the implications of Marcel's youthful experience. But he does not foreclose his own drama, for it is the adult Swann we see, not the adult Marcel. Swann is, in many ways, Marcel's avatar, but one who failed to respond to a vocation which he apprehended but dimly. His failure indicates the possible failure of Marcel. Later in the novel, Marcel will follow the emotional, the social and even the aesthetic patterns set by Swann. He will take love to be the ultimate reality; he will seek reality in the pseudo-sanctifications of social success; he will falsely attribute to external objects a reality which can only derive from within the self; and he will doubt the reality of his vocation. But Marcel finally goes beyond these failures to the redemption of *Le Temps retrouvé*.

Un Amour de Swann, like *Combray*, suggests that things and people are not what they seem to be, that life is a progress from illusion to illusion, interspersed with rare moments, to which we pay too little heed, when a hawthorn tree in bloom or a haunting phrase from a sonata briefly capture our attention with the promise of a new insight into reality. Charles Swann's story ends with the recognition that he has made a ludicrous mistake—the woman he thought he loved so deeply was not his type at all: he was not the self he thought himself to be. With this paradigm of failure in mind, we return to the evolution of the self of Marcel, in his adolescence.

Noms de Pays: le Nom, returning to the first-person narration of Marcel, links the two preceding sections together. It shows Marcel, in his relationship with Gilberte, Swann's daughter, performing emotional arabesques similar to those of Swann in his affair with Odette. It shows the endless illusions and self-deceptions that accompany the development of a love-affair. It also offers a new view of Swann. The adjunct of family life in Combray, and the tormented hero of *Un Amour de Swann* is once more transformed, as Gilberte's father, into a 'personnage historique', whose mysterious profile lends a new and magical dimension to the umbrella counter of a fashionable department store (I, 414).

In this third part, the accumulated vocabularies of the first two parts flow together and gain in richness, while repeated evocations of different scenes and different times—times spent at Venice, Doncières or Balbec—remind the reader that all the scenes and incidents are artificial cross-sections in the indivisible and complex flow of Marcel's life.

The volume ends with a return to the present of the narrator—'this year, November'—when he revisits the Allée des Acacias in the Bois de Boulogne where, as a child, he had so eagerly waited to see Mme Swann go by. Mme Swann, like her husband, is a Protean figure. She has already figured as Swann's socially unacceptable wife, glimpsed in the park at Tansonville: she has briefly appeared as Uncle Adolphe's 'dame en rose', and she has been the Odette de Crécy beloved of Swann, before appearing as Gilberte's elegant mother. Thinking back to the lovely moments spent in the Allée, Marcel shows us Odette in a multiple vision. Through the eyes of the child, she smiles with the 'bienveillance d'une Majesté', while through the eyes of the older narrator, she displays 'la provocation d'une cocotte'. While the awed child marvels at her elegance, a less impressionable bystander comments drily: 'J'ai couché avec elle le jour de la démission de Mac-Mahon.' It is a complex vision, compounded of Marcel's view as a child, his later reflections on that naïve view, and his view 'now', as a mature man. We end again (as in *Combray*), in that indefinite 'now', with the mature Marcel revisting the Allée in nostalgic mood, longing to recapture what is no longer to be found.

Marcel acknowledges defeat. The world he seeks has vanished. The elegant carriages have been displaced by cars, and a motley collection of mediocre persons has been substituted for the irreplaceable ladies who adorned his youth. The impression of the absolute and the necessary has been ousted by the perception of the contingent and the sham. Time past is not to be recaptured in places or in things, and *Du Côté de chez Swann* ends with the painful—but fruitful—recognition that the search, this time at least, is vain, for 'les maisons, les routes, les avenues, sont fugitives, hélas, comme les années' (I, 427).

With these three beginnings Proust introduces us to a truly original view of a shifting world, seen by changing eyes from diverse positions.[3] The normal chronology of the novel, the 'then, now, and hereafter', is abandoned in favour of a more complex chronology, corresponding not to clocks but to inner necessities. We have, in this first volume, three introductions to the novel: one starting from the childhood of the narrator, one that goes back into his pre-history (making that childhood merely a point on a more extended line), and one in which the childhood and the pre-history meet and intermingle. After this triple introduction, we have acquired the vision and perceptions native to the narrator, the

[3] Cf. F. C. Green, *The Mind of Proust* (Cambridge University Press, 1947), p. 413: 'Marcel . . . surveys his past from many changing sites of the self, from different states of soul.'

points of reference and 'vocabulary' of his experience. We are ready to embark on the narrator's long pilgrimage.

The three parts of *Du Côté de chez Swann* thus seem to outline the artist's first skirmishes with time and truth. The attempt to recapture Combray is put to flight by the intruding light of morning. The history of Swann's love-affair ends in the recognition that he has wasted precious years of his life. *Noms de Pays: le Nom* ends similarly in defeat. Truth is not to be conquered by mere recollection, by love, nor by imagination. The triple defeat, however, has its positive side, for Marcel has at least learned that he must seek elsewhere the path that will lead him to the elusive truth which transcends time.

3. *Signposts*

Even in the midst of his struggles and apparent defeats Marcel has certain intimations, whose full scope and significance he does not yet grasp. In *Combray*, there are two major incidents which produce such intimations, and serve as signposts to Marcel's later discoveries. The first is the tasting of the *madeleine*, and the consequent restoration of the past through involuntary memory. The second is Marcel's reaction to the church-steeples at Martinville, and the translation of that experience into words. Marcel learns from both of them. He learns from the *madeleine* incident the role of involuntary memory in the kind of creation he has in mind, though the lesson will only mature when reflection on this and similar incidents has led him to greater understanding. From the steeples of Martinville, Marcel receives confirmation of his artistic vocation through the act of creation itself. These 'signposts', with their mysterious coded messages, are deliberately placed at significant positions in the novel. The first, the *madeleine*, provides a way out of a world of shadows into a world of greater substance and solidity. The second, the steeples of Martinville, indicates the path of artistic creation at a point when the young Marcel, in failing to respond to the challenge of the world, is in danger of losing a part of himself.

The 'madeleine'[1]

It is to a world of shadows that Proust introduces us in the opening pages of *Combray*. These pages reflect the loss of identity associated with sleep, and the instability of the 'kaléidoscope de l'obscurité' which surrounds the narrator with successively remembered scenes. When the narrator's mind focuses on his bedroom at Combray, he recalls a room lit by the flickering images of the magic lantern, and the restlessness of the external picture is reinforced by the emotions of Marcel the child, anxious, fearful and guilt-ridden. Marcel identifies his mother with the unhappy Geneviève de Brabant, heroine of the lantern-slides, while the crimes of the villain Golo make him examine his own conscience with more scruple. The early pages of Proust's novel thus draw attention to the instability of the forms of the world before Marcel has seized their solidity. One way of seeing Marcel's central preoccupation in the novel is to say that he seeks to replace this apparent anarchy with unity, and to find form, solidity and identity in what seem at first mere fleeting shadows.

A recurrence of the magic lantern image, in the final volume of *A La Recherche du Temps perdu*, underlines its significance. It repeats and clarifies the distinction, anticipated in the early pages of the novel, between the thin superficial world of the magic lantern and the volume and density of reality. During a reception given by the Guermantes, at the end of *Le Temps retrouvé*, Marcel finds his fellow-guests changed by the action of time. For a while, the guests have the puppet-like quality of Golo. Then Marcel looks more closely at one of them, M. d'Argencourt, and makes a discovery that he will put into effect in the novel he has yet to write. It is that people exist *in time*: it is only by replacing them in the dimension of time that we can properly see them. To restore life to these 'vieillards fantoches', he declares, 'on était obligé de les regarder en même temps qu'avec les yeux, avec la mémoire' (III, 924). Marcel sees the guests

[1] On the structural importance of the *madeleine*, see Richard Macksey's essay in *Proust, A collection of critical essays*, ed. R. Girard (New Jersey, Prentice-Hall, 1962), and Jean Rousset's article reprinted in *Les Critiques de notre temps et Proust*, ed. J. Bersani (Paris, Garnier, 1971).

as shadows projected by time's magic lantern.[2] In order to restore depth to these figures who seem mere 'poupées', 'il fallait lire sur plusieurs plans à la fois, situés derrière elles et qui leur donnaient de la profondeur . . .' (III, 927). Looking at this from the point of view of Marcel the narrator, we can say that at a particularly bleak moment of despair and self-doubt, he is here illuminated by a perception of fundamental importance to his novel. In the writing of that novel, he will represent his discovery concretely by creating first the flickering world of the magic lantern, and by moving from this to that seeing not merely with the eye but with the memory, which, he has realized, is the way to give substance and solidity to the world's restless surfaces.

In the opening pages of the novel, Marcel also contrasts the limited world available to the conscious memory with the richer world available only through the combined action of *mémoire involontaire* and art. The only part of Combray which is accessible to Marcel's conscious memory centres around the 'drame du coucher'. Having disobeyed parental law by staying up for his mother's goodnight kiss, Marcel is appalled at his father's indulgence, which recognizes the child's weakness as 'un mal involontaire'. Marcel is filled with guilt and remorse towards his mother: 'Il me semblait que je venais d'une main impie et secrète de tracer dans son âme une première ride et d'y faire apparaître un premier cheveu blanc' (I, 39). It is as if Golo had again attacked the château of Geneviève de Brabant, and now repented of his crime.

We can see here that guilt towards his mother which is such a marked feature of Proust's thought. He had disappointed her by his indolence, by his assiduous attendance at fashionable salons, by his failure to make a career for himself, and by his homosexuality which he had to keep hidden from her. Reflected in the magnitude of the task Proust set himself in his novel is his passionate desire to redeem himself, and make of Golo-Marcel, the insubstantial puppet, a Marcel worthy of his mother's selfless love.

The bed-time drama plays, in relation to the *paradis perdu* of Combray, a role similar to that of the Fall in the Garden of Eden: it is the revelation

[2] 'Des poupées baignant dans les couleurs immatérielles des années, des poupées extériorisant le Temps; le Temps qui d'habitude n'est pas visible, pour le devenir cherche des corps et, partout où il les rencontre, s'en empare pour montrer sur eux sa lanterne magique. Aussi immatériel que jadis Golo sur le bouton de porte de ma chambre de Combray, ainsi le nouveau et si méconnaissable Argencourt était là comme la révélation du Temps, qu'il rendait partiellement visible' (III, 924).

of a weakness which leads to exclusion from a world of innocence. If, however, Marcel is able to resuscitate other parts of his life at Combray, he may rediscover other selves less irretrievably flawed than the guilty child which alone he remembers. As a result of the *madeleine* and the action of involuntary memory, Combray is indeed restored, and along with it, new aspects of Marcel.

Voluntary memory, in Proust's view, only brings back what the intelligence has classified and ordered. It does not reach the essence of things as they exist in 'la vraie vie'. It does not reach that complex vitality of things which Elstir, for instance, tries to render in his paintings, stripping away the categorizations of intelligence.[3] Proust tries to restore the original experience in all its complexity, with its distortions, gaps and optical illusions. Voluntary memory is an inadequate tool for such a purpose, for it is too much the slave of intelligence, too subject to the organizing power of 'raisonnements'. Voluntary memory reduces us, in the words of Samuel Beckett, to the level of the tourist—'whose aesthetic experience consists in a series of identifications, and for whom Baedeker is the end rather than the means'.[4] It is only through the action of involuntary memory that the past can truly be recalled, and involuntary memory is usually awakened by sensation.

There are, in *A la Recherche du Temps perdu*, many notable examples of 'mémoire involontaire', of which the *madeleine* is the first and most striking. Others are the steeples of Martinville, echoed by three trees near Balbec; a musty smell in a public lavatory of the Champs-Elysées, recalling the garden-room of Uncle Adolphe at Combray; a hawthorn hedge near Balbec, recalling the hawthorns of Combray; the vivid recollection, when Marcel's grandmother is dead, of the moment when she helped him off with his boots in the Grand Hotel at Balbec; uneven flagstones in the Guermantes courtyard, repeating a similar sensation experienced in the Piazza San Marco in Venice; the clanking of a spoon, recalling the clank of a railwayman's tool; the sensation of a stiffly-starched napkin recalling a starched towel at Balbec; and the novel, *François le Champi*, loved by Marcel as a child, and seen again in the Guermantes library. These various triggers of Marcel's involuntary memory allow him an insight into the 'moi permanent' which subsists

[3] 'Elstir tâchait d'arracher à ce qu'il venait de sentir ce qu'il savait; son effort avait souvent été de dissoudre cet aggrégat de raisonnements que nous appelons vision' (II, 419).

[4] Samuel Beckett, *Proust* (New York, Grove Press, 1931), p. 11.

beneath the changing selves he adopts in the course of his life. They stimulate involuntary memory which, as Howard Moss puts it, 'induces perception and is not a repetition but a revelation'.[5]

It is sensation that reawakens the past, and particularly, for Proust, the sensations of smell and taste. The whole of Combray is saturated in the scent of hawthorn and lilac, scents from which Proust was in later years cut off by his asthma. Yet, years later, he tells us, in a haunting phrase, he often smells through the rain, 'l'odeur d'invisibles et persistants lilas' (I, 186). The fragrance of the invisible lilacs of Combray in that Mallar-méan phrase is the sign of the tough durability of the most apparently evanescent impressions: it sums up the survival within the mind of things—or people—long absent or dead. Not only their survival, but the continuance of all their rich evocative powers. As the 'unheard melodies' of Keats 'pipe to the spirit ditties of no tone', so Proust's absent lilacs perfume the spirit with unearthly scents; and fill it with joy.

The power of such sense-impressions is indicated when Marcel reflects: 'quand d'un passé ancien rien ne subsiste, après la mort des êtres, après la destruction des choses, seules, plus frêles mais plus vivaces, plus immatérielles, plus persistantes, plus fidèles, l'odeur et la saveur restent encore longtemps . . . à porter sans fléchir, sur leur gouttelette presqu' impalpable, l'édifice immense du souvenir' (I, 47). And this indeed is what we encounter in the case of the *madeleine*, out of whose taste comes Combray and the restoration of a forgotten epoch of the narrator's life.

The moment Marcel tastes the *madeleine* dipped in tea, he tells us, 'je tressaillis, attentif à ce qui se passait d'extraordinaire en moi'. He feels a mysterious and unaccountable joy, accompanied—characteristically—by a desire to discover its source. For despite the importance Proust grants to intuitive perception and sensation, he is no simple intuitionist: the products of his intuitions are constantly sifted by his analytical intelli-gence. After repeating the sensation, with no further illumination, Marcel realizes that what he is looking for is not in the *madeleine* but in himself: 'Il est clair que la vérité que je cherche n'est pas en lui mais en moi.' He now turns inward to continue his search, and realizes that it is not merely a matter of search, but also of creation: 'Chercher?' he asks, and answers himself: 'pas seulement: créer.' It is partly a matter of seeking and

[5] Howard Moss, *The Magic Lantern of Marcel Proust* (London, Faber and Faber, 1963), p. 108: pages 112, 113 of this volume offer a fuller list of involuntary memories than I give here.

finding, and partly a vital act of creation. Passive sensation is not enough; an act of imagination is required to find the metaphor, which will raise the *im*pression into an *ex*pression.

Repeated efforts to trace the source of his feeling convince Marcel that somewhere a visual image is attached to the taste of the tea, but they do not tell him what it is. When he has given up the effort, and let his mind wander back to the ordinary preoccupations of the day, the memory suddenly unfurls in his mind. Like those Japanese paper flowers that twist and turn and open out in water, so the flowers of the old garden, the water-lilies and the lilac, the people and the church of Combray, 'tout Combray et ses environs, tout cela qui prend forme et solidité, est sorti, ville et jardins de ma tasse de thé' (I, 48).

This experience is a model of the way in which Proust explores the sensations deposited in him by childhood experience, and finds the metaphors—that is, creates the world and the figures of Combray—which translate that experience. For Marcel the narrator, the restoration of Combray and the resurrection of a lost self are a foretaste of the realizations he achieves in *Le Temps retrouvé*, but they are incomplete. Marcel is unable, at this stage, to account for the extraordinary joy the recollection has given. Later, he will understand the source of that joy: the recollection of Combray is a decisive proof that the Marcel who earlier experienced the rich reality of Combray has not disintegrated in his passage through time. He still endures within the frame of the older disillusioned Marcel, and is still capable of the same unreasoning joy in the vivid existence of himself and the world.

The *madeleine* thus offers Marcel a foretaste of a discovery which will ultimately make possible a victory over time the destroyer. The involuntary memory can awaken a self momentarily freed from the restrictions both of the present moment and of the moment remembered—a self which links the two together in a sphere of heightened consciousness. The 'veritable being', as Georges Poulet puts it, 'is he whom one recognizes not in the past, nor in the present, but in the rapport which binds past and present together'.[6] Marcel in such moments is no longer a mere slide in time's magic lantern: he acquires depth and density. His consciousness is briefly freed from the limits of his own self-knowledge, from the demands of self-assertion, and the boundaries of his present mood and will. Through involuntary memory, the past is restored—not

[6] Georges Poulet, 'Proust and Human Time', in *Proust, A collection of critical essays*, ed. R. Girard, p. 170.

the past as seen and ordered by the present Marcel, but the 'lost' past, in all the richness and variety that had escaped his conscious attention.

The *madeleine* incident is therefore of vast importance in the structure of Proust's novel, for it represents concretely the belief that underpins the whole novel: that there is within each individual an inner world which is his own. It is his personal creation, a creation in which all his experience coexists organically. Proust's task was to find the means to express that inner world of whose existence he was convinced. He does so by a system of analogy and metaphor. Marcel is the analogue of Proust himself, and Marcel's experiences, emotions, disappointments and aspirations are analogues of Proust's. The *madeleine* is the analogue by which Proust expresses his faith in the unique enduring identity of the self and its vast creative energy. For the narrator Marcel it is an experience whose full scope and significance he cannot yet fully appreciate, though its effect—the recollection of Combray—bears implicit witness to its power.[7]

The steeples of Martinville

Operating the trigger of involuntary memory, the *madeleine* makes possible a second phase in the evocation of Combray—the evocation of its 'forme et solidité'. It resurrects the long summer days, the Sundays of *tante Léonie*, and the walks along the two ways—the one leading past Swann's house, and the other to the château of the Guermantes family. The Swann side, through the person of Swann, prefigures the distractions of love and worldly ambition in the life of Marcel, and outlines the artist *manqué* he was long in danger of becoming. The Guermantes side holds both the lure of snobbery, and the artistic aspiration that finally overcame it. It is on the Guermantes side that Marcel has his first experience of a successful translation of reality into art, through his description of the steeples of Martinville, observed from Dr Percepied's carriage. And this experience, as I suggested earlier, is strategically placed. It occurs when Marcel is dejected at his lack of talent, and acutely aware of his failure to seize what the world seems simultaneously to offer and conceal.

Marcel tells us that his eye was often caught by objects which gave

[7] Cf. Germaine Brée, *Marcel Proust and Deliverance from Time* (New York, Grove Press, 1955), p. 23: 'The very existence of Combray . . . is enough to counterbalance all the pessimistic judgements of the world formed by the narrator. . . .'

him a special sense of pleasure, and which seemed to hide 'quelque chose qu'ils m'invitaient à venir prendre et que malgré mes efforts je n'arrivais pas à découvrir' (I, 178). This is what happens when he sees from the carriage the two steeples of Martinville, followed by the steeple of Vieuxvicq. Marcel feels that something more lies behind the image he sees. But, as in the *madeleine* incident, the 'something' which they seem to hide lies not in them but in himself. It is by exploring and expressing his own impressions that Marcel captures at once the essence of the steeples and himself. It is through the steeples that Marcel expresses himself, and through himself that he expresses the steeples. It is not the outer or physical features of things that matter—it is how they exist in us, and we in them.

The experience of the steeples is echoed, later in the novel, in the sight of three trees, observed from the carriage of Mme de Villeparisis (I, 717). In the trees Marcel instantly recognizes a recurrence of something, but he cannot find the source of the memory, or grasp what they seem to be trying to say to him.

They seem, however, to warn him:

> Ce que tu n'apprends pas de nous aujourd'hui, tu ne le sauras jamais. Si tu nous laisses retomber au fond de ce chemin d'où nous cherchions à nous hisser jusqu'à toi, toute une partie de toi-même que nous t'apportions tombera pour jamais au néant. (I, 719)

The trees, like the steeples of Martinville, draw attention to those privileged moments when Marcel perceives dimly the shadow of 'la vraie vie', though his actual life, like the carriage in which he sits, bears him speedily away.

The steeples show how the child reacts to his intimation of a message in the physical world which requires to be translated. Despite his momentary fascination, Marcel was ready, when the carriage unexpectedly reached the church, to put away his impression, along with a number of other things—ferns, or pebbles—briefly noticed but not explored. In the light of the later incident of the trees, we may observe that what he is here tempted to discard includes 'toute une partie de lui-même'. The coachman, however, is not talkative, and Marcel begins, after all, to recall the steeples and their movement. He formulates his impressions in words, and this act of translation gives him an intense and exhilarating pleasure. The words give rise to thoughts he did not have before, and the pleasure of seeing the steeples is greatly intensified, for this is a moment when Marcel reaches out beyond what Germaine Brée characterizes as 'intellectual sloth' to 'precision of language, the expression of the real quality of an individual's contact with the world in which he lives'.[8] Marcel sees the steeples again, black now the sun has gone down, then briefly once more in the distance, and they are gone. The child then writes down the passage which the mature Marcel later transcribes into his narrative.

What the steeples mean to Marcel is revealed in a series of images. They are birds on the plain far off: then the Vieuxvicq spire moves off, leaving the other two playing and smiling. They all rush to meet the carriage, which is only just able to stop in time. When the carriage moves off, the three spires stand waving goodbye, moving out of each other's way, to let the others see. They are three flowers painted on the sky, three legendary maidens, timidly searching out their path in the growing darkness. At last they join together in 'une seule forme noire, charmante et résignée' (I, 180).

We see here successive spatial and temporal relations explored, an interrelating of different moments, aspects and distances. The steeples are seen separate, together, moving this way and that, and finally merging into one form. As the impression of physical distance is abolished by the tricks and changes of perspective, so physical time is abolished by the tricks and changes of an imagery which creates the effect of simultaneity. The steeples seem both here and there, both then and now. They have achieved a density derived from the 'eye of memory' and the perspective of time. In a similar way, the characters of Proust's novel, moving this way and that, changing yet identical with themselves, finally merge into one complex form. We may see, as Georges Poulet suggests, a fundamental feature of Proust's treatment of movement in this creation of unity and continuity out of fragments and multiple aspects.[9]

The steeples may be seen as a spatial metaphor of a temporal process. As Marcel moves through the incidents and experiences of his life, he sees things in many lights and from many angles. The mobility of this viewpoint causes changes of impression: as the steeples seem birds, flowers, or legendary maidens, so Mme Verdurin seems a bird, and M. de Palancy a fish. As the steeples change as Marcel moves in space, so Odette, as he moves in time, is variously *la dame en rose*, Odette de Crécy, and Mme

[8] Germaine Brée, *Marcel Proust and Deliverance from Time*, p. 6.

[9] v. Georges Poulet, 'L'Espace Proustien' in *Entretiens sur Marcel Proust*, ed. G. Cattaui and P. Kolb (Paris, Mouton, 1966), p. 8.

Swann. As the steeples merge with one another, so do the fragments of Odette combine to make one complex figure. In the journey of Marcel's life, things once distant are sometimes very near, and things that seem inseparable from him retreat into the distance. The apparent change and movement of the steeples in the perspectives of space parallel the change and movement of events and people in the perspectives of time.[10] The change and the movement here are the result of the narrator's motion, which creates new relationships. In Marcel's life, the shifting relationships are even more complex, since events and people also have independent motion.

In this first successful translation of reality into art, we may observe many of the salient features of Proust's art in the novel. It is characteristic of him to work, as here, from an original and often confused sensation towards a complex reconstruction of the various elements of that sensation, producing what Professor Macksey has called 'a kind of achievement of simultaneity through analogy'.[11] It is also characteristic of him to unify the diverse elements by making them cohere in the subjectivity of the narrator. Further, just as Marcel does with the moving spires, so Proust, in his novel, lends intensity and volume to the characters and events by superimposing various temporal and spatial frames.

This incident thus offers the first evidence of the reality and value of Marcel's vocation. During a great part of his lifetime, Marcel doubts the existence of his talent, does not know where to find his subject, and even doubts the value of literature itself. But if the *madeleine* is the analogue of Proust's faith in the creative power of the inner world, the steeples of Martinville are the analogue by which Proust affirms the conquest of his own doubts, and declares his ultimate faith in art as the instrument which can deliver and make manifest that hidden virtuality. Through art, time the destroyer may yet become time the creator.

[10] See Germaine Brée's discussion of Proust's *Figaro* articles of 1907, one of which, exploring the 'dislocations of space' caused by viewing the world from the window of a moving car, was the source of the Martinville spires passage. Professor Brée suggestively links this exploration of changing spatial perspectives with Proust's comments, in the other articles, on the 'telescopic' eyes of old people which seem to move so rapidly through time, and on the power of the telephone to cancel distance. *The World of Marcel Proust* (London, Chatto and Windus, 1967), pp. 93–5.

[11] Richard Macksey, 'The Architecture of Time: Dialectics and Structure', in *Proust, a collection of critical essays*, ed. R. Girard, p. 120.

4. The World in Time

Space and time
Are not the mathematics that your will
Imposes, but a green calendar
Your heart observes . . .

R. S. Thomas, *Green Categories*

Time is not for Proust the subject of an intellectual theory marginal to his work but a concept that deeply influenced the very structure of that work. His own reflections on his experience coincided with a pre-occupation of his time, that issued notably in the works of the philosopher Henri Bergson.[1] From the very beginning of the novel, we can hardly help being aware of the curious time-schemes to which Proust introduces us. He tries to recreate for us not chronological time as observed by clocks and calendars, but the fluid structures of time as it is experienced—that time which Bergson termed 'durée'. We all know that in internal time, the length of minutes varies: experienced time is elastic. An hour may seem a day, and a month may flit past like a week. Internal time can elide great slabs of external time, and construct vast distances between things that chronologically succeed each other rapidly. Proust explores in his novel not only time's elasticity, but the creative and destructive powers generated by that elasticity.

At the very beginning of the novel, we are propelled into an internal world of reminiscence and reflection in which present and past intermingle, and where normal chronology has no sway. The temporal framework from which the narrator's voice addresses us is not defined: it is only 'sometime'. The first sentence: 'Longtemps je me suis couché de

[1] For discussion of Proust's debt to Bergson see, for instance, L. A. Bisson, 'Proust, Bergson and George Eliot' (*Modern Language Review* XL, p. 104); R. Champigny, 'Proust, Bergson, and other philosophers', in *Proust, a collection of critical essays*, ed. R. Girard; Floris Delattre, *Bergson et Proust: accords et dissonances* (Paris, Albin Michel, 1948); F. Fabre-Luce de Grusen, 'Bergson et Proust', in *Entretiens sur Marcel Proust*, ed. G. Cattaui and P. Kolb.

bonne heure', paradoxically combining the most immediate form of the past with 'longtemps', instantly suggests the absorption of great stretches of the past into the moment in which the narrator speaks. The scarcely glimpsed contours of that implicit 'now' dissolve when the voice slides into the continuous tense of the imperfect: 'Mes yeux se fermaient . . . je n'avais pas le temps de me dire "Je m'endors".' The intrusion of the voice speaking in the present tense reminds us that this past time was once immediately present, and suggests that it is still accessible. From imperfect we move to pluperfect: 'Je n'avais pas cessé en dormant de faire des réflexions sur ce que je venais de lire. . . .' He goes on to explore the confusion of the moments between waking and sleep, when thoughts belong half to the world of reality and half to the fantasy world of dream. The location of the narrator at the moment of his narration remains undefined, even when he describes his attempts to relate himself to the world about him. He asks, in the past tense, the very question which arises *now* for the reader, with regard to the temporal location of the narrating voice: 'What time is it?'—'Je me demandais quelle heure il pouvait être.' In this indefinite past, lacking even the anchor of a relation to a defined present, the narrator evokes a state of mind in which neither time nor place have clear contours: 'J'entendais le sifflement des trains qui, plus ou moins éloigné, comme le chant d'un oiseau dans une forêt, relevant les distances, me décrivait l'étendue de la campagne déserte.' The world evoked here is decisively a mental construction, stimulated, however, by the real whistles of passing trains. It is the quality of the sounds the sleeper hears that creates the distances, and the distances evoked by the sounds create an imaginary landscape. In that imaginary landscape a figure emerges, responsive to the call of the trains: 'le voyageur se hâte vers la station prochaine; et le petit chemin qu'il suit va être gravé dans son souvenir. . . .' We are caught up in the present of an imaginary traveller, moving to a station which lies ahead of him—in the future. The reference to the traveller's memory anticipates a point at which his present will have moved through the future and into the past of his memory. The remembrance of the path on which he now moves will be due to the excitement of new places, the memory of recent conversations, the farewells he has just made—and also to his anticipation of 'la douceur prochaine du retour'.

Proust has created here a composite in which the present of the imaginary traveller (evoked in the framework of the past of the narrator) is itself suspended between past and future. In the future, the present will be the past, but the past will still be virtually present through the power of memory. Thus in this deservedly famous first paragraph, Proust introduces the reader to the temporal complexity of a novel in which the present of the narrator is 'sometime' and his geographical location 'somewhere', but in which all times and all places within his experience coexist and interact. We can, as readers, identify with the traveller, setting foot on the path over which the narrator has long before us travelled. We can also see in the imaginary traveller the emergent figure of Marcel, through whose journeyings and experience we shall enter analogically the inner world of Proust himself.

As the narrator is never precisely located in time, his future is never imaginable; we literally shouldn't know where to begin, for where does his 'present' end? The future involved in the narration is already past for the narrator. Time here is circular; it is the meeting place of past, present and a specious future. If we ask: what does Marcel do, after the final scene of *Le Temps retrouvé*? we can only answer: he writes the book he has discovered how to write. The narration itself is his future. Time, in the inner world, is not linear; 'Un homme qui dort tient en cercle autour de lui le fil des heures, l'ordre des années et des mondes' (I, 5). Through art, the sleeper may deliver into daylight the richness of a world that thrives on darkness and solitude. Through art, Proust finds an accommodation of the conflicting demands of complexity and coherence, of the rational and the irrational. It is a matter of showing, in the whirling of hours, the 'thread' that links them, and in the wheeling of places, the 'order' the mind creates and imposes upon them.

Out of the circle of years and worlds, Proust creates a novel in which time never ceases visibly to flow by. The past shapes and colours both present and future, and more than that, the past itself changes in response to changes of focus or understanding in the narrator. The 'thread' of the narrator's consciousness gives unity to the diverse episodes. Within that 'fil', Marcel's mother, Mme de Guermantes, Gilberte and, later in the novel, Albertine, are all facets of the woman Marcel loves. Throughout the novel these strands are woven together, and the images converge, so that at the end of *Sodome et Gomorrhe*, when Marcel is filled with jealousy over Albertine, he feels the same 'atmosphère hostile, inexplicable, comme celle qui montait jadis jusqu'à ma chambre de Combray, de la salle à manger où j'entendais causer et rire avec les étrangers . . . maman qui ne viendrait pas me dire bonsoir; comme celle qui avait rempli, pour Swann, les maisons où Odette allait chercher en soirée d'inconcevables joies' (II, 1121). Times and tenses meet, woven together into the thread of Marcel's inner reality.

The world of Combray, as Marcel presents it, is soaked in an awareness of the flow of time. A great part of Combray's charm consists in its age —its old streets, bearing the names of saints, its 'vieille hôtellerie de l'Oiseau flesché', and, above all, its ancient church. Within the confines of Marcel's bedroom, history reverberates into the present, as the magic lantern produces images of a Merovingian past which is, however, linked with the present through the *duchesse de Guermantes*. For the duchess is a descendant of Geneviève de Brabant, the heroine of the lantern slides. The *curé* invokes episodes of Combray's history in his etymological dis- cussions, and these episodes become a part of Combray's legend. They form part of that 'tradition orale déformée et vivante' which, Marcel tells us, still inspires Françoise, as it once did the medieval sculptor of the church.

Laden with the pluperfect of its history, Combray evolves in the melancholy tense of the imperfect, appropriate to the continuous tradi- tion and ritual evident in the smallest details of the family life of Marcel's childhood. Even the fact of having lunch early on Saturday, so that Françoise can get to the nearby market, becomes not only a family joke but a family ritual. The question: 'Qui cela peut-il être?' which attends Swann's ringing of the visitors' bell is another ritual faithfully observed. By its continuous identity within an organized form, ritual confers on everyday events a historical volume. It makes moments so time-laden that they seem to carry the past into the present and the future. Time as meaningless succession is converted by ritual into time as creative repetition.

Ritual, tradition, history, memories, change, age, decay, forgetfulness, habit—all these are the common products of time reflected in Proust's pages. But Proust also presents time in more concrete terms—it is, as it were, materialized. It is made visible, for instance, in the dried linden flowers out of which *tante Léonie* makes her *tisane*. Marcel observes the shrivelled flowers, the twisted stems, and brittle leaves. Marvelling at their change, he nonetheless recognizes with joy that 'c'était bien des tiges de vrais tilleuls, comme ceux que je voyais avenue de la Gare, modifiées, justement parce que c'étaient non des doubles, mais elles- mêmes et qu'elles avaient vieilli' (I, 51). When these dried-up blossoms are used for the *tisane*, their scent and savour are released. Despite all the evidence of time's action upon them, they have maintained the identity of their inner being, and they thus provide an implicit anticipation of the moment when Marcel rediscovers his same self within the withered dried-up soul he seems to have become.

'Time' is an abstraction, but Proust finds it concretely present in many objects and events. Time may be experienced in terms of physical sensation, as when Marcel, reading in the garden in Combray, hears the chiming of the church-clock. The clock strikes the hour into the blue sky:

> Et à chaque heure il me semblait que c'étaient quelques instants seulement auparavant que la précédente avait sonné; la plus récente venait s'inscrire tout près de l'autre dans le ciel et je ne pouvais croire que soixante minutes eussent tenu dans ce petit arc bleu qui était compris entre leurs deux marques d'or . . . (I, 87)

Time here is a 'petit arc bleu', miraculously containing sixty minutes, though for Marcel it has had a much shorter duration.

Time is materialized again in the windows of the church, with their 'vieillesse argentée' (I, 60) and in the smoothness of the *bénitier*, polished by the fingers of generations of worshippers. The weight and power of time are also made visible in the stone tombs around the choir. They are no longer inert hard matter. Time has made them soft, and made them flow like honey, carrying a flowery Gothic capital from one tomb to another, contracting an already elliptic Latin inscription, joining letters previously separated, and separating others (I, 59).

The 'action of time' is not here a mere metaphor: we see it polishing, burnishing, softening, pushing, pulling and actively changing the features of things and of people. In its vivid representation of the organic force of time, the church seems to Marcel 'un édifice occupant . . . un espace à quatre dimensions—la quatrième étant celle du Temps' (I, 61). It is tempting to draw an analogy between the church, laden with the emblems of successive epochs, and the memory of Marcel the narrator. Time will work on his mind as it worked on the tombs, joining what once was separate, separating what seemed joined—creating new and constantly-changing patterns in the ciphers engraved by experience. Like the church, Marcel's memory may be seen as an 'édifice' which traverses 'des époques successives d'où il sortait victorieux', and from the tower of his narrating consciousness, as from the tower of Saint Hilaire, 'on embrasse à la fois des choses qu'on ne peut voir habituellement que l'une sans l'autre' (I, 106).[2]

Proust's complex consciousness of time is reflected in another way through what we may call changes of narrative perspective. There are frequent reminders that the narrator is himself subject to time. Marcel underlines the provisional nature of the 'present' viewpoint by inter-polations which serve to show it as only one angle of vision within a wider perspective, a perspective in which Marcel is actually situated 'bien des années plus tard'. Or he reminds us, with phrases like 'je sus bientôt, comme on le verra' (I, 418), that a future, already past for the narrator, still lies ahead in the narration. We see, for instance, through the lighted windows of Montjouvain, a scene between Mlle Vinteuil and her lesbian friend, and we are offered a very brief intimation of the atrocious role this scene will later play in the relationship between Marcel and Albertine: 'le souvenir de cette impression devait jouer un rôle important dans ma vie' (I, 159). The 'future' qualifies the 'present' just as the past does.

Sometimes our attention is drawn to mistakes Marcel makes, as when he imagines that Swann would scoff at the pleading note sent by the child to his mother—'or, au contraire, comme je l'ai appris plus tard, personne aussi bien que lui peut-être n'aurait pu me comprendre' (I, 30). Sometimes we are encouraged to make the same mistakes, by sharing the limitations of the 'present' viewpoint, as when we hear in Combray the gossip about Mme Swann and Charlus. Future revelations will cast a new light both on the characters concerned and on their relationship.

Such shifts of perspective keep the reader constantly aware of time as a further dimension in the novel. The narrator, early in the novel, indicates both the creative and the destructive force of time when, commenting on changes in the external world, he adds: 'En moi aussi bien des choses ont été détruites que je croyais devoir durer toujours et de nouvelles se sont édifiées, donnant naissance à des peines et à des joies nouvelles que je n'aurais pu prévoir alors' (I, 37). We thus see Marcel's life in a complex perspective, for he shows us not only what he saw and experienced at a specific time, but how his vision altered in response to later events and experience, and even beyond that, the vision afforded by the mature and

[2] Georges Poulet draws attention to the significance of this passage in his essay 'Proust and Human Time' in *Proust, a collection of critical essays*, ed. R. Girard, p. 176.

detached vantage-point of a narrator who fully recognizes the instabili-
ties of perspective.

The novel makes us aware that each conclusion is but a provisional
one. *Un Amour de Swann* ends with Swann's realization that he has wasted
years of his life on a woman not his type; but we next meet that appar-
ently-discarded woman as Swann's wife, and mother of Gilberte. The
value and significance of events are subject to fluctuation, yet nothing
disappears without trace. Our inner self is more loaded with time's
wealth than we can easily know.

Marcel's task is to restore to his own life, and to the lives of those who
inhabit it, that wealth which is not perceptible save in an extensive
temporal perspective. In *Le Temps retrouvé*, when Marcel has at last
discovered the kind of novel he wants to write, he says of it:

> J'y décrirais les hommes, cela dût-il fes faire ressembler à des êtres
> monstrueux, comme occupant dans le Temps une place autrement
> considérable que celle si restreinte qui leur est réservée dans l'espace,
> une place, au contraire, prolongée sans mesure. . . . (III, 1048)

Only in time can they reveal their multiplicity and their volume. It is
the place which people occupy in Marcel's evolving consciousness, their
place in the shifting patterns of his memory, which gives them their
changing but distinctive features. The three figures of Swann, as he
appears at non-successive phases of his life in the three parts of *Du Côté
de chez Swann*, offer a striking instance of the way Proust's characters
acquire volume.

Proust's concept of time as an active element in human life could
scarcely fail to exercise a profound influence on his concept of character.
In *La Fugitive*, Proust writes that just as there is a geometry in space, so
there is a psychology in time, in which the calculations of a plane psychology (by analogy with plane geometry) would not be accurate. So we
move with Proust from a flat psychology to a psychology in time, in
which emotional attitudes are not consistent and people do not have fixed
characters. Marcel sums it up in the statement: 'nous ne sommes pas un
tout matériellement constitué' (I, 19). People change in themselves, and
change further in response to the views of others: 'notre personnalité
sociale est une création de la pensée des autres' (I, 19). We cannot predict
the emotions and moods of others, and we cannot foresee our own. We
change beyond our calculations. The Marcel in love with Gilberte looks
forward to meeting her in the Champs-Elysées, but once there, both he

and she are changed in the new situation. The loving Marcel and the loved Gilberte are displaced by the playmates Marcel and Gilberte, caught up in a new relationship. The new pleasures deriving from the new situation offer little to the desiring soul of Marcel, for 'ces plaisirs nouveaux ... n'étaient pas donnés par la fillette que j'aimais, au moi qui l'aimais, mais par l'autre, par celle avec qui je jouais, à cet autre moi ...' (I, 404). Proust shows that our ordinary conceptualizations of people and their characters could only be appropriate to static puppets, and are thoroughly inadequate to living people who change, age and constantly move in time. No character can be fixed and known: Swann as Gilberte's father, is a 'personnage nouveau', and no longer the family guest at Combray. In the world of relationships, 'la réalité est ... quelque chose qui n'a aucun rapport avec les possibilités' (I, 363). Since people are subject to profound changes when in the grip of profound emotions, they are unpredictable and mysterious—often to themselves. Swann's whole mode of life changes in response to his passion for Odette: 'Tant une passion est en nous comme un caractère momentané et différent qui se substitute à l'autre et abolit les signes jusque-là invariables par lesquels il s'exprimait' (I, 235).

Swann's life is so totally engulfed by his passion for Odette that not only does he think and act differently, but he fears any cure of the anguish of his love-affair as he might fear death itself (I, 300). The self and the state of passion become temporarily identified. And the emotions which cause such profound changes are not themselves fixed or continuous entities. Love itself is not one state but a succession of states, and jealousy similarly: 'notre amour, notre jalousie ... se composent d'une infinité d'amours successifs, de jalousies différentes et qui sont éphémères, mais par leur multitude ininterrompue donnent l'impression de continuité, l'illusion de l'unité' (I, 327).

The self, then, is a multiple being, subject to disparate pressures. Where character is concerned, Proust replaces solidity and unity by change and multiplicity. As Martin Turnell puts it: 'The classical novelists were convinced that in spite of his changing moods, man was essentially *one*. Proust was equally convinced that he was *many*.' But Proust is not frivolously attacking the unity of the human person. On the contrary, his work, as Turnell goes on to insist, outlines 'a more profound conception of the self which would give him a better chance of reaching the elusive "vraie vie" and revealing its mysteries'.[3] Beneath the fragmenta-

[3] Martin Turnell, *The Novel in France* (Penguin Books, 1962), p. 394.

tion of the self exists a 'moi permanent', an 'être extra-temporel' who can be rediscovered in certain privileged states, brought about by the action of the involuntary memory—as in the case of the *madeleine* dipped in tea, whose taste brings back to Marcel the long-forgotten world of Combray.

The whole of Proust's novel tends to the construction of that extra-temporal reality as it exists in Marcel's 'moi permanent'. The endeavour involved a new treatment of spatio-temporal relations, a treatment which would show the effects of time and distance on the mind, and the effects of mind on time and distance. For it is clear that inner time and inner distance do not obey the same rules that govern physical time and distance. They have their own laws. Mental time and distance may separate things joined in physical time and space. The fuchsias of Mme Loiseau spread themselves over the façade of the church, but remain obstinately separate from the church: 'entre les fleurs et la pierre noircie sur laquelle elles s'appuyaient, si mes yeux ne percevaient pas d'intervalle, mon esprit réservait un abîme' (I, 63). A mental distance separates them. Similarly the *côté de chez Swann* and the *côté de Guermantes* are separated less by their 'distances kilométriques' than by 'la distance qu'il y avait entre les deux parties de mon cerveau où je pensais à eux' (I, 135). Inner time and distance may also join together things separated physically, for time and space are swallowed up into internal space-time. When the view of distant steeples in Paris strikes the eye of the middle-aged narrator who has lost his way in a strange part of the city, it arouses in him a dim sense of 'terres reconquises sur l'oubli' (I, 67). Memories of Combray and of pebbles on a beach converge, and he stands staring: 'je cherche encore mon chemin, je tourne une rue . . . mais . . . c'est dans mon cœur' (I, 67). One might say the whole novel represents this effort to find the way, not to the steeples of the here and now, but to the 'terres reconquises' where stand the steeples of the heart.

5. A View of Life

Cette perpétuelle erreur, qui est precisément la 'vie', ne donne pas ses mille formes seulement à l'univers visible et à l'univers audible, mais à l'univers social, à l'univers sentimental, à l'univers historique, etc. . . . Nous n'avons de l'univers que des visions informes, fragmentées et que nous complétons par des associations d'idées arbitraires, créatrices de dangereuses suggestions.

(III, 573)

We are not what we think we are and the world is not what we take it to be. Such is the message of Proust's view of the world, and stated thus bluntly, it has all the thudding banality that derives from transposing the work of a great novelist into generalized formulae. But such simplifications will, nevertheless, allow us to look at his work with an eye to its moral implications.

Life is a comedy—sometimes a tragedy—of errors. We make mistakes about everything, from the names of casual acquaintances to the nature of our deepest feelings. We rarely see what we are doing, and often assume that others are equally blinded. Proust often uses such mistakes to comic effect. To his wife's reproach: 'Voyons, ne dîtes pas du mal d'Odette', M. Verdurin replies with a hypocrisy characteristic of humanity at large: 'Nous ne disons pas du mal d'elle, nous disons que ce n'est pas une vertu ni une intelligence' (I, 228). A more serious revelation, accompanied by the comment 'tant les gens les plus sincères sont mêlés d'hypocrisie' (I, 149) is made when Marcel's parents and Vinteuil together fall to lamenting Swann's unfortunate marriage, in the name of principles which, they seem to imply, are not contravened at Montjouvain. Yet Vinteuil is at the very same time dying of grief at the vice of his daughter.

If people did not make such mistakes, they could not posture as they do—and then fall victim to their own posturing. Léonie has to remember not to use phrases like 'when I woke up' since her daily life is postulated on the notion that she never sleeps. Mme Verdurin is similarly affected by her protestation that music affects her so profoundly as to make her ill: 'Peut-être . . . à force de dire qu'elle serait malade, y avait-il des moments où elle ne se rappelait plus que c'était un mensonge et prenait une âme de malade' (I, 207). A good deal of what people believe about themselves is nonsense in the service of self-flattery. Odette believes that she loves and admires disinterestedness, but 'ce qui parlait à son imagination, ce n'était pas la pratique du désintéressement, c'en était le vocabulaire' (I, 245). Odette's belief is typical of human self-deception, in that it allows her to preserve the noble role she has allotted herself. Swann, disillusioned with the Verdurins who have excluded him from their society, and driven a wedge between him and Odette, instantly feels a 'mission' to remove Odette from so base a milieu. But he does not acknowledge his desire to remove her from a milieu which has suddenly proved hostile to himself. Legrandin similarly has no idea he is a snob: he finds motives for frequenting his social superiors which are not the motives of a snob at all. Blind to ourselves, 'nous ne connaissons jamais que les passions des autres' (I, 129).

These moral observations are made by explicit and often generalized comment from the narrator, who, by virtue of detachment and hindsight, can accurately observe the behaviour of his fellows. By maintaining a distance between his 'moraliste' persona and his role as protagonist, Marcel is able to subject his own character and experience to a similar moral scrutiny. In the experience of the child Marcel, Proust is thus able to reveal Marcel's moral character in the actual process of formation. The child's quick sensibility is caught in the act of adapting to a life where suffering and cruelty are accepted and tolerated. Marcel is made miserable when his great-aunts tease his grandmother by persuading her husband to drink the cognac forbidden by the doctor. But, 'déjà homme par la lâcheté, je faisais ce que nous faisons tous . . . quand il y a devant nous des souffrances et des injustices: je ne voulais pas les voir' (I, 12). He already foresees a time when, behind the shield of laughter, he will give his allegiance to the persecutor.

Marcel's immediate reaction to the sight of Françoise savagely slaughtering a chicken is a desire to drive her away from the house. But there is an overriding matter of personal interest. Who, then, would make the delicious treats in which Françoise specializes? Who, indeed, would serve such succulent chickens? An accommodation with an imperfect world is clearly necessary: 'ce lâche calcul, tout le monde avait eu à le faire comme moi' (I, 122). Thus we learn to accommodate our experience, but what we experience is itself carefully filtered so that we may avoid too painful a confrontation with reality. When Legrandin, in the grip of a snobbishness quite unsuspected by Marcel's family, cuts

Marcel and his father dead, Marcel's father is very reluctant either to acknowledge the fact or see any significance in it. The child is more immediately perceptive, for he is still an apprentice in that art of evading reality which his elders have mastered.[4] Swann skilfully contrives to evade full consciousness of his suffering at the waning of Odette's affection. He makes a detour in his room to avoid the cabinet in which Odette's early love token—the chrysanthemum—is enclosed. And he makes a detour in his mind to avoid the place where the memory of his 'jours heureux' lies locked. It is only the Vinteuil Sonata, bringing back the lost moments of happiness sharply to his mind, that overcomes his 'si précautionneuse prudence' (I, 322). We live, the narrator suggests, in shells of self-protective illusion: 'les faits ne pénètrent pas dans le monde où vivent nos croyances' (I, 148).

When we can no longer resist the fact, we develop a further power of distortion or diminution by which we succeed in absorbing it in our world. In this way, we learn to live with things we should otherwise regard as monstrous and intolerable. The child accepts the suffering of his grandmother and the cruelty of Françoise. M. Vinteuil, a loyal supporter of conventional moral principles, accepts the installation of his daughter's lesbian friend at Montjouvain, and the narrator makes this general comment:

> Il n'est peut être pas une personne, si grande que soit sa vertu, que la complexité des circonstances ne puisse amener à vivre un jour dans la familiarité du vice qu'elle condamne le plus formellement—sans qu'elle le reconnaisse d'ailleurs sous le déguisement de faits particuliers qu'il revêt pour entrer en contact avec elle. (I, 148)

The disguise of reality is its particularity. The abstract detestation of vice is inadequate to the particularities of a given situation. All the efforts we make to apprehend reality intellectually, by abstracting, categorizing and classifying, leave us vulnerable. They do not prepare us for the Protean and complex figures of a reality that does not correspond to abstract notions. Swann's emotions are lacerated not by 'unrequited love' but by a faded flower, a gilt letterhead or a snatch of music.

The grasping of reality is further complicated by the difficulty of apprehending the reality of the self. How indeed can one adequately apprehend a reality at once so manifold and so unstable? One of the

4 See Rosalie Taylor, 'The Adult World and Childhood in Combray' (*French Studies*, January 1968).

first things Marcel notices about himself is his discontinuity: he observes 'ces états qui se succèdent en moi, . . . et vont jusqu'à se partager chaque journée . . . contigus, mais si extérieurs l'un à l'autre, si dépourvus de moyens de communication entre eux, que je ne puis plus comprendre, plus même me représenter, dans l'un, ce que j'ai désiré, ou redouté, ou accompli dans l'autre' (I, 183). Marcel is not alone in this. Swann's father, grief-stricken after his wife's death, is nonetheless capable of a sudden upsurge of joy. We are all discontinuous: we forget ourselves in the most precise and literal sense. Swann, in the grip of a perception of Odette's resemblance to the Botticelli Zéphora, 'oubliait qu'Odette n'était pas plus pour cela une femme selon son désir' (I, 224), and goes on to have his most serious love-affair with a woman who is really 'not his type'.

Life, in Proust's view, is compounded of such errors. Indeed, in Proust's novel, as Roger Shattuck succinctly puts it: 'Error, optical illusion, provides the material out of which truth must emerge . . .'.[5] Sometimes the errors are superficial—a mispronunciation such as that which makes Mme Sazerat 'Mme Sazerin', or a malapropism like Françoise's use of 'parenthèse' meaning 'parenté'. More often, however, they reflect human disharmony in its many forms. The lack of understanding between one being and another is presented vividly in the early pages of Combray, on the occasion when the great-aunts so notably fail to express their gratitude to Swann for his gift. They also demonstrate a singular capacity for total deafness when the conversation moves on to subjects they regard as too frivolous or commonplace. What is of extreme interest to the grandfather is of none at all to the sisters, and the patterns of this comic scene foreshadow later episodes which reveal in more sombre colours the gulf that separates one human being from another.

But human beings frequently do not recognize this gulf. Most of the time they are content to imagine the rest of the world to be in tune with themselves. Yet they are all divided in both trivial and fundamental ways by differing desires and differing scales of value. Value is subject to variations which are not merely subjective but positively eccentric. The beautiful antiques, which Swann as a connoisseur has collected about himself, seem to Odette a rather disgraceful accumulation of broken old furniture and faded carpets, quite unworthy of his social position. But social prestige itself is variable. Odette's notions of what is 'chic' would

[5] Roger Shattuck, Proust's Binoculars (London, Chatto and Windus, 1964), p. 98. See also Jean-Yves Tadié, Proust et le roman (Paris, Gallimard, 1971), Chapter II. 'Points de vue et perspectives'.

seem the last word in vulgarity in the elegant salons that Swann so gracefully adorns.

We tend, however, Proust suggests, to assume that values are absolute, and that the standards we accept are Standards. We do not make sufficient allowance for the enormously different notions other people have, nor for the unsuspected significances our conduct may have for other people. Various sequences in the novel are made of chains of such misunderstanding . . . Marcel, as a child, imagines the mind of others (as he suggests we all do) as a sort of 'réceptacle inerte et docile, sans pouvoir de réaction spécifique sur ce qu'on y introduisait' (I, 79). Since he is himself filled with delight at having met 'la dame en rose' at his uncle Adolphe's apartment, he assumes it can cause only interest and delight in others. He therefore tells his parents about the incident, despite his uncle's clear hint that he had much better not. Marcel is then shocked at the serious repercussions of this tiny piece of information. Angry at Marcel's being introduced to a *cocotte*, his parents quarrel with Adolphe. Later, when meeting his uncle in the street, Marcel is too ashamed to respond politely to his uncle's greeting. Adolphe assumes that Marcel is withholding his salutation in accordance with instructions from his parents, and he never forgives them for it. He dies without ever seeing them again.

Even where greater harmony prevails about standards of conduct and values, people's moods rarely coincide. The exultant greeting of Marcel, enchanted by the autumn colours, meets only a gruff and surly response from a passing peasant, and Marcel reflects that 'les mêmes émotions ne se produisent pas simultanément chez tous les hommes' (I, 155). At the very moment when he rushes affectionately to embrace his parents, they, having just learnt of some minor offence he has committed, turn to scold him. There is no emotional co-ordination, even between those supposedly linked by bonds of affection. How rarely Odette answers the desires of Swann's mood, and how often indeed, while he is so preoccupied with her, she forgets him utterly! While Swann longs to see her after her return from Pierrefonds, she, not sparing him a thought and finding herself alone, goes to the theatre. Marcel tries to tell himself that Gilberte is as concerned to see him as he to see her. But she expresses delight and joy at those special outings with her mother, which, since they keep her away from the Champs-Elysées, fill him with anguish.

When we are not faced by the problems of discordant emotions, we are often bedevilled by ignorance, prejudice or preconception. The family at Combray, knowing Swann as 'le fils Swann', remains com-

pletely blind to Swann's dazzling social life. When they give an important dinner, they may well ask Swann's advice on some practical matter,
or request a recipe for a sauce, but they would not think of inviting him.
One of the great-aunts refers, complacently, to 'people you and I are
never likely to meet, M. Swann', while Swann sits there with, more than
likely, a letter from the Prince of Wales in his pocket. Swann himself is
guilty of a similar failure of vision when he totally fails to recognize, in
the Vinteuil of Combray, Vinteuil the composer whom he reveres.
Marcel, when he at last meets Bergotte in the flesh, will also observe a
vast gulf between the silver-haired bard he had imagined and the man
with a nose like a snail that he actually encounters. In his insistence on the
gulf that separates the artist from the man, Proust seems indeed to be
making an implicit appeal. Knowing too well the limitations of Proust
the man, he covertly reminds us to recognize and judge him not by the
ephemeral features of his human life, but by the enduring achievement
of his art.[6]

It might seem that love might be the way human beings could sometimes escape from this encounter of subjective eccentricities. Proust's
view of love, however, is not encouraging. Effectively, it throws us back
once more upon the self, rather than forward towards reciprocity. Love
is merely a state of mind in the lover, a state which can be aroused by
such diverse stimuli as the insolent gesture of Gilberte at Tansonville or
the kindly glances of the Duchess in church at Combray. If the one
provokes by its seeming scorn, the other lures by its seeming promise.
The gestures in themselves are insignificant to the point of being inter-
changeable, and we learn later in the novel that Marcel has misinterpreted
both. There was no affability in the eye of the Duchess, and Gilberte's
gesture was in fact a lewd invitation. It is what Marcel projects on to
these figures that makes them a focus for his affections.

In Swann's affair with Odette we see the complex dance of these two
generators of love—invitation and rejection. Swann finds himself in a
lover's situation thanks to Odette's pursuit of him. When once *in* the
situation, he gradually acquires the attributes of the lover. Proust refers
to the process as one of catching up in a known dance—'nous avons assez
l'habitude de cette musique pour rejoindre tout de suite notre partenaire

[6] Milton Hindus, *A Reader's Guide to Marcel Proust* (London, Thames and
Hudson, 1962), p. 42. stresses 'the self-conscious emphasis' Proust gives to
'the lesson that man as a social being and man as an immortal soul capable
of divine aesthetic creation are incommensurable concepts'.

au passage où elle nous attend' (I, 197). Odette is not at all the type of woman who normally attracts Swann. On the contrary, she seems to him thin, pale, haggard and tired-looking, whereas he prizes the fresh, plump, rosy young girl, like the *ouvrière* who continues to satisfy his physical needs during the early stages of his affair with Odette. Odette, however, acquires prestige in his eyes by her resemblance to the Botticelli painting, and he enjoys, furthermore, the flattery of being pursued by Odette, who, he imagines, is much sought after. He fabricates an Odette quite other than the *cocotte* known to others. For him she is 'une femme difficile'. Swan therefore ambles, as it were, into a situation where, without realizing it, he comes to rely more and more on the reassuring presence of Odette.

What stimulates a new and more powerful attachment is Odette's absence when Swann arrives one evening at the Verdurins—having stayed too long with his *ouvrière*—and finds her already departed. At this moment the anguish (which is the emotion by which Proust tends to identify love) begins. When Swann eventually finds Odette, after searching desperately in the Paris streets and cafés, he experiences the vast relief of anguish comforted, and this 'apaisement' which derives from the presence of Odette becomes vital to him. He is now dependent on her soothing presence, torn by jealousy in her absence, and tormented by suspicion. Odette's moments of forgetting him 'servaient mieux à lui attacher Swann, que toute sa coquetterie. Car ainsi Swann vivait dans cette agitation douloureuse qui avait déjà été assez puissante pour faire éclore son amour' . . . (I, 295).

Swann is now in the grip of a passion which derives from the mechanics of his own character rather than from the responses of hers: 'La personne même d'Odette n'y tenait plus une grande place' (I, 308). Swann has become one with his passion; his identity is swallowed up in it: it has changed his life, his character, and his outlook. 'Comme on dit en chirurgie', the narrator laconically comments, 'son amour n'était plus opérable' (I, 308). Even the Verdurin clan, which would ordinarily have been beneath Swann's social notice, seems to him—thanks to the presence of Odette—a distinguished and splendid milieu. We are made to observe the full extent of Swann's mistake when Proust uses, to express Swann's view of the Verdurin 'salon', that recurrent and highly-charged term, 'la vraie vie': 'Quel charmant milieu, se disait-il. Comme c'est au fond la vraie vie qu'on mène là' (I, 248). In the context of the novel it is rather like suggesting that the Verdurins keep the Holy Grail on their mantelpiece. And it indicates that Swann has indeed lost sight of the true life he ought to be pursuing and has mistakenly turned his quest towards tawdry substitutes. Marcel, in turn, will do the same, pursuing 'la vraie vie' in eroticism and social success. But Marcel, unlike Swann, will learn to acknowledge his error, and have time enough to rectify it.

If we look at Marcel's love for Gilberte we find a similar pattern. He is looking, in her, for a reflection he has himself projected on to her. Bergotte plays the role that Botticelli played for Swann, and the Champs-Elysées takes the place of the Verdurin salon. The agate marble replaces Odette's chrysanthemum, and the alternations of hope and despair are similar. We see the same pattern of obsessed lover and indifferent loved one—a pattern subsumed succinctly in the telling phrase with which Proust refers to the act of love: 'l'acte de la possession physique—où d'ailleurs l'on ne possède rien' (I, 234).

It is a disheartening picture of love, and, we may feel, a distorted one. It is arguable that Proust's inordinate craving for affection—represented already in Marcel's relations with his mother—made it impossible for him to find in love any real satisfaction for his needs. He would always want more: an impossible total contact and communion with the loved one. Such a communion and contact are possible only in the imagination. In Marcel's later love-affair with Albertine, we see Marcel's moments of highest satisfaction achieved in the contemplation of Albertine asleep; the loved one's necessary presence without the elusive consciousness that evades embrace.

It is clear then that in Proust's view we are all at the mercy of ourselves —those selves we neither comprehend nor control, and which lead us to the pursuit of illusions whether they be of love or of social success.

Perhaps the fundamental human mistake, the fundamental mistake for the artist certainly, is the failure to perceive our own reality. We look to the world outside for things that we can find only in ourselves. We look, in things, for 'le reflet que notre âme a projeté sur elles'. We fail to see that it is the place of things in the pattern of our internal world that gives them their strange beauty, their mysterious resonance. We thrill to the sound of a sonata or the colours of a sunset, and imagine that by buying the record, or gazing at more sunsets, we can gain something further.[7]

[7] 'Certains hommes seuls se penchent sur l'inexplicable sillon tracé en eux. . . . Beaucoup se détournent. Et, se consolant de ne pas chercher à savoir, aiment la chose qui a creusé le petit sillon . . .' (Proust, quoted by Maurice Bardèche in *Marcel Proust, romancier*, p. 255).

But it is only when we pause and discover the nature of the thrill itself, when we find what meaning, what points of reference it has in our experience—in short, when we find the metaphor—that we begin to take possession of the beauty we glimpsed and enjoy the happiness we suspected.[8] In Proust's view (the view of an artist) we achieve true reality only by creation. It is by expressive acts alone that we break down the barriers of our solitude and impose order on our constant flux.

In Marcel's visit to the Allée des Acacias at the end of *Noms de Pays: le Nom* we see a clear instance of the self searching in the external world for a reflection of itself. The middle-aged narrator is seized by the desire to see again what he once loved, and he returns to the avenue with the same ardour that had driven him years before to await the passing of Mme Swann. But he has made the fundamental mistake: what he is looking for is not in the Bois de Boulogne. He needs to make the recognition previously made about the taste of the *madeleine*: 'Il est clair que la vérité que je cherche n'est pas en lui, mais en moi' (I, 45). His attachment to the Allée des Acacias is an instance of the fetishism that survives when faith is dead—it is a superstitious attachment to a totemic object. The avenue is changed beyond recognition; the elegant carriages, the beautiful society ladies, have all vanished, and Marcel gazes in horror and disillusion at 'le vide inhumain de la forêt désaffectée (I, 427). *Le Bois* has become *un bois,* and Marcel understands 'la contradiction que c'est de chercher dans la réalité les tableaux de la mémoire' (I, 427). This is at least a first step towards the realization that it is only by exploring his inner world that he will be able to recapture the happiness he pursues and find that beauty of which things merely serve to remind him.

Through the figure of Swann, and through the interpolations of the mature Marcel, Proust is able to express the understandings that underpin the entire novel more directly than is possible in terms of the experience of the youthful Marcel. We already know, through Marcel as a child, of the enormous prestige of the artist, through the child's reverence for the writer Bergotte. But we learn more about the nature of art through Swann's experience of the Vinteuil sonata. We see the artist as a seeker out of new truths when Swann finds in Vinteuil an 'audace aussi géniale peut-être . . . que celle d'un Lavoisier, d'un Ampère, l'audace d'un Vinteuil expérimentant, découvrant les lois secrètes d'une force

[8] 'Ce que nous arrivons à lire dans le grimoire fleuri, ceci est le livre vrai dicté par la réalité, le nôtre . . .' (Proust, quoted by Maurice Bardèche in *Marcel Proust, romancier,* p. 256).

inconnue . . .' (I, 351). We see art, the product of this 'audace', as the source of 'un bonheur noble' (I, 210) and see it as a real and autonomous entity. The little phrase, for instance, for Swann, 'existait latente dans son esprit au même titre que certaines autres notions sans équivalent comme la notion de lumière, de son, de relief, de volupté physique . . .' (I, 350).

The action of the phrase on Swann, its capacity for reawakening memories which had vanished from his mind, is an echo of the *madeleine*, of the *clochers de Martinville*, and a foretaste of those other privileged moments Marcel experiences. The effect of the phrase on Swann is to return him to himself, causing him great pain but preparing the way for new understanding. Just as the *madeleine* unveils dark areas in Marcel's mind, and just as the uneven paving-stones encountered in *Le Temps retrouvé* restore Marcel to himself, so the little phrase of the sonata performs a great service for Swann. It is the service rendered, Proust tells us, by certain great artists, who, 'en éveillant en nous le correspondant du thème qu'ils ont trouvé', are able to demonstrate 'quelle richesse, quelle variété, cache à notre insu cette grande nuit impénétrée et décourageante de notre âme que nous prenons pour du vide et pour du néant' (I, 350).

Proust precisely tries to awaken within us 'le correspondant du thème', and to make 'chaque lecteur . . . le propre lecteur de soi-même. L'ouvrage de l'écrivain n'est qu'une espèce d'instrument optique qu'il offre au lecteur afin de lui permettre de discerner ce que, sans ce livre, il n'eût peut-être pas vu en soi-même' (III, 911). What the *madeleine* does for Marcel, and the little phrase for Swann, Proust's novel can more fully do for his readers, if they but seek to find what corresponds in themselves to the themes he has developed. Whatever the apparent emptiness or sterility of the soul within us, Marcel may become an analogue for the reader, as well as for Proust, of the potent virtuality of the inner world.

Proust uncovers the mechanisms of egocentric individuals, propelled by desire and vanity. He uncovers too the apparently rigid patterns derived from heredity and early experience—those patterns that make us ceaselessly imitate ourselves. Yet despite the repetitive twitches of our puppet-lives, we each have within us a life that we uniquely create in our passage through time. And it is that life that Proust seeks to express and communicate in his novel.

6. The Search for 'La Vraie Vie'

> . . . *la vraie vie* . . . *cette vie qui, en un sens, habite à chaque instant chez tous les hommes aussi bien que chez l'artiste.*
>
> (III, 895)

What gives Proust's novel its unique character is above all its combination of a tough-minded analytical realism with a synthesizing poetic vision. It is that vision, expressed through style, that transforms the cold facts of a closely-observed social world into the elements that compose the organic world of a single human experience. The individual consciousness records, registers, compares, contrasts and analyses the features it encounters, using its resources of sensibility and intellect. But it also does far more: it creates. It composes, out of the fragments of perceived reality, a rich and interrelated world, imposing harmony and order where life seemed to offer mere confusion, and imposing identity on a self apparently doomed to discontinuity and fragmentation

For the 'realism' that annotates the facts and surfaces of the world, Proust substitutes the search for a 'reality' that corresponds to the 'vraie vie' hidden in each individual consciousness. He discards the meticulous exercises in imitative realism practised by such writers as the Goncourt brothers—whose work he effectively parodies in *Le Temps retrouvé*. In *Un Amour de Swann*, a 'romancier mondain' puts in an appearance at Mme de Saint-Euverte's reception. He has come equipped for his task, with a monocle stuck in the corner of his eye—'un monocle, son seul organe d'investigation psychologique et d'impitoyable analyse' (I, 327). 'Whatever are you doing here?' someone asks him. With an important and mysterious air, and rolling his 'r's, he replies: 'J'observe.' This is no doubt the kind of observer Marcel has in mind when he speaks of 'un observateur que ne voit les choses que du dehors, c'est à dire qui ne voit rien' (I, 390).

Marcel does not despise observation—far from it[1]—but clearly finds it inadequate. In himself he sees only an intermittent observer, one more concerned with the 'essence générale' than the surface. Yet this intermittent observer does not crudely neglect the surface in favour of the essence. Marcel combines the precision of superficial observation with a search for the general laws of human behaviour. He sees the particular with an eye to the general: the particularity of Mme Verdurin, for instance, is allied to the typical characteristics of the *parvenu* snob, and to the general characteristics of an epoch. In his creator's hands, Marcel is a considerable social analyst, sensitive to the fine nuances of social reactions to such diverse phenomena as sexual deviations, the Dreyfus affair, the emergence of new salons or the First World War. Part of the story he recounts is the disintegration of the aristocracy and its capitulation to the bourgeoisie. In that story, he is attentive to social details in the careers both of individuals and of social groups. He captures not only the language and gesture of individuals but the character and style of social groups, and beyond this, the interaction of the two. He shows the effect of the individual on the group (the *duchesse de Guermantes* and her salon) and the effect of the group on the individual (as seen in Odette's imitation of Mme Verdurin's manners and tones).

Realism begins with an attention to surfaces. But as we recognize the meaning of these surfaces, we penetrate to what is hidden beneath them. For instance, as we peer with Marcel through the lighted windows of Montjouvain, we see Mlle Vinteuil placing carefully beside her the portrait of her dead father (I, 160). We may see, if we wish, a lesbian responding to a sadistic impulse to desecrate the image of her father: she will see her companion spit upon the portrait, and make it the witness of their guilty pleasures. But we also see, in the very movements Mlle Vinteuil makes, a precise repetition of the movements of her father when Marcel saw him placing on the piano the piece of music he hoped to play to Marcel's parents. And when she draws her companion's attention to the portrait, she uses the very words used by Vinteuil about the music-

[1] There is a vigorous defence of Proust's observation in J. F. Revel, *On Proust* (London, Hamish Hamilton, 1972), though the author dismisses too high-handedly Proust's use of metaphor and his search for 'la vraie vie': 'Whatever his own views, it is not when he is being metaphorical that Proust is a great writer; it is not when he is being poetical that he is original and has something to teach us; it is when he is being realistic, when he is the narrator and chronicler that he is the great writer' (p. 160).

sheet. At the same time, this whole scene registers itself uniquely in Marcel's mind to become a focus for his later anguish about Albertine's suspected lesbianism, and a focus too for his feeling of guilt towards his grandmother. Later in the novel, Marcel's grandmother, aware of her approaching death, decides to have a photograph of herself taken, as a souvenir for her grandson. To hide her already disfigured face, she wears a big hat, and takes great pains to ensure the success of the picture. Marcel metaphorically spits on the image of his grandmother, by seeing in her action a selfish and unexpected vanity which upsets him and makes him spoil all her pleasure in her benevolent action. Marcel therefore later associates the vividly-remembered scene of Montjouvain with his guilt towards his grandmother. Albertine's reawakening of the scene in his imagination seems to him the punishment of that guilt.

This brief scene is characteristic of Proust's methods: it shows meticulous observation of gesture, expression, and movement. It then draws attention to the various 'lois générales' which lie behind them: the force of heredity, reproducing the father in the daughter; the forces of virtue and filial affection meeting the forces of 'le monde inhumain du plaisir' to generate Mlle Vinteuil's sadism. Beyond the surface realism, and the capturing of the 'essence générale', we see also how the scene becomes a significant cipher in the language in which Marcel will understand his own relation to Albertine, and to his grandmother.

Each surface detail is a key that unlocks a meaning, for observations made over time reveal patterns and significances. When Odette smiles her Botticelli smile, we see instantly the discomfort of the liar; when Cottard smiles his 'sourire conditionnel et provisoire', we see the self-protection of a humourless naïf, insensitive to tones of voice. In Saniette's speech-defect, we find 'une qualité de l'âme, comme un reste de l'innocence du premier âge qu'il n'avait jamais perdue. Toutes les consonnes qu'il ne pouvait prononcer figuraient comme autant de duretés dont il était incapable' (I, 203). The surface details are seen as fragments of an elusive human whole.

To observe details and generalize from them may seem simple, but it is a process full of traps. Conventional notions and categories always stand greedy-mouthed to gobble up the fruits of observation. Proust leaves them hungry. Proust's form of realism demands precision, and the search for the exact phrase or image which describes the thing observed. Description, under these conditions, becomes analysis. Love, for instance, under this scrutiny, breaks down into a succession of diverse emotions.

'Sadism', as we see it in the Montjouvain scene, becomes a battlefield of conflicting desires. Even death, so understandably more appealing as an abstraction, becomes something tightly anchored in physical reality.[2]

Proust is always concerned to find beneath the immediate phenomena some 'essence générale' which only emerges when one seizes upon the similarity between apparently disparate things. 'La vérité', Proust writes in *Le Temps retrouvé*, 'ne commencera qu'au moment où l'écrivain prendra deux objets différents, posera leur rapport . . . et les enfermera dans les anneaux nécessaires d'un beau style' (III, 889). He attempts to find the common elements and thus create a coherent and analogical view of the world. On the one hand, we have the coherence of general laws deduced from lengthy observation: laws of heredity, of self-protection, of self-flattery and self-deception—the laws by which we all tend to repeat ourselves, reproducing over and over again the same patterns in our response to the world. On the other hand, we have a system of analogy and association by which all our diverse experiences are interrelated, a system linking the hawthorns of Combray with the sea at Balbec, the scene at Montjouvain with Albertine and Marcel's grandmother.

To move from 'realism' in the conventional sense to the kind of reality Proust was seeking, many obstacles must be overcome. The writer is also an actor on the social stage, and likely therefore to be absorbed, like Swann, in occupations which allow little time for reflection. And the practical activities of life encourage two things which further hamper the artist's endeavour: forgetfulness and habit. Forgetfulness Proust calls 'un si puissant instrument d'adaptation à la réalité'. Without it, life would be intolerable: we need to forget. Habit is the 'aménageuse habile mais bien lente' without which life would constantly be astonishing and disturbing. Dulling our consciousness of the familiar, habit releases our attention for what is new, or what we have selected as genuinely interesting. But most remedies are poisonous if taken to excess. If the work of 'habitude' and 'oubli' were never interrupted, we might forget even those fragments of experience by which we recognize ourselves, and habit might create a

---

[2] 'Bien souvent la pensée des agonisants est tournée vers le côté effectif, douloureux, obscur, viscéral, vers cet envers de la mort qui est précisément le côté qu'elle leur présente, qu'elle leur fait lourdement sentir et qui ressemble beaucoup plus à un fardeau qui les écrase, à une difficulté de respirer, à un besoin de boire, qu'à ce que nous appelons l'idée de la mort' (I, 82).

dull world in which no mystery or strangeness reawakens our sensibility.

Classification is to the understanding what habit is to life: an orderly system which prevents our being swamped by diversity. But we pay for the convenience of the system by a blindness to what lies outside it. The artist must overcome the distortions of the categorizing intelligence if he is to explore the richness of experience. One can thus see why involuntary memory is of such importance to Proust: it can escape the domination of consciousness, will, purpose, habit, forgetfulness, and self-deception. It can elude the control of the intelligence, and give us back the sharp sensations of our experience, linking what we are to what we have been.

In the preface to *Les Plaisirs et les Jours*, Proust makes this interesting revelation:

> Quand j'étais tout enfant, le sort d'aucun personnage de l'histoire sainte ne me semblait aussi misérable que celui de Noé, à cause du déluge qui le tint enfermé dans l'arche pendant quarante jours. Plus tard, je fus souvent malade, et pendant de longs jours je dus rester aussi dans 'l'arche'. Je compris alors que jamais Noé ne put si bien voir le monde que de l'arche, malgré qu'elle fût close et qu'il fît nuit sur la terre.[3]

In this image of Noah seeing the world from the closed Ark, we learn that for Proust, life has more reality re-created in the mind, than under its immediate impact: 'la véritable réalité n'étant dégagée que par l'esprit, étant l'objet d'une opération spirituelle, nous ne connaissons vraiment que ce que nous sommes obligés de recréer par la pensée, ce que nous cache la vie de tous les jours' (II, 770). We see an instance of this in *Combray*, where Marcel's most powerful awareness of summer comes not in the heat of the sun, but in the cool shade of the room where he lies reading. He is able to re-create summer in his mind from a few precise stimuli—flies buzzing, and the grocer hammering crates outside. Undistracted by the diverse events and myriad sensations of a summer day, he is able to enjoy 'le spectacle total de l'été, dont mes sens, si j'avais été en promenade, n'auraient pu jouir que par morceaux' (I, 83).

Proust's concern with inner reality does not mean he is insensitive to external reality. On the contrary. Proust was an accomplished mimic, quick to catch at the revealing gesture, the identifying tic or mannerism, the telling modulation of tone. Swann's tone, as he declares his prizing, above all things of magnanimity, betrays 'cette légère émotion qu'on

[3] *Jean Santeuil*, preceded by *Les Plaisirs et les Jours*, ed. P. Clarac and Y. Sandre (Paris, *Pléiade*, 1971), p. 6.

éprouve quand, même sans bien s'en rendre compte, on dit une chose non parce qu'elle est vraie, mais parce qu'on a plaisir à la dire et qu'on l'écoute dans sa propre voix comme si elle venait d'ailleurs que de nous mêmes . . .' (I, 249). This acutely perceptive faculty allows Proust to present a multitude of characters so vividly that we recognize their tone immediately, and perceive the gestures that characterize them—we note the involute pedantry of Bloch, the pretentious preciosity of Legrandin, the affected anglicisms of Odette, the atrocious puns of Cottard, the ironic quotation-marks affected by Swann, the self-conscious daring of M. Biche, or the curious enunciation of the pianist's aunt, deliberately blurred to conceal her lack of grammar. Not only peculiarities of language, but oddities of expression and tone, of movement and gesture, are precisely seized. The accuracy of Proust's observation often creates richly comic scenes, as when he etches a hilarious and unforgettable picture of Legrandin, in the grip of his snobbery, offering to Marcel and his father, as they pass by, 'une prunelle enamourée dans un visage de glace' (I, 125), or shows us the *princesse des Laumes* at a concert, beating time with her fan—'mais, pour ne pas abdiquer son indépendance, à contretemps' (I, 331).

But what Proust seeks in external realities is what they may reveal of an inner and essential truth. He is aware that truth does not lie necessarily in careful compilations of spoken words, aware that 'la vérité n'a pas besoin d'être dite pour être manifestée, et qu'on peut peut-être la recueillir plus sûrement . . . dans mille signes extérieurs, même dans certains phénomènes invisibles, analogues dans le monde des caractères à ce que sont, dans la nature physique, les changements atmosphériques' (II, 66). Marcel searches out the tiniest details of observable behaviour and relates them to inner patterns. In the coy gesture with which Mme Blatin rotates her neck and produces the ticket for her seat in the Champs-Elysées, he sees the gesture of a *coquette* eager to please her admirer, pointing to her corsage with the comment: 'Vous reconnaissez vos roses' (I, 406). The essence of the woman is revealed in her tiny affected gesture.

When Marcel's grandmother surreptitiously removes some of the training-wires from the roses as she goes by, Marcel sees the gesture of 'une mère qui, pour les faire bouffer, passe la main dans les cheveux de son fils que le coiffeur a trop aplatis' (I, 14). In both cases, a tiny movement is illuminated by an analogy which reveals its significance— Marcel's grandmother is the eternal mother, caring only for what is free and natural, while Mme Blatin is the eternal *coquette*, concerned only to make a flattering impression. Tiny indications, in Proust's treatment, lead to large conclusions.

Perhaps one of the most striking instances of this seizing of the 'signe extérieur' occurs in a scene at the Verdurin household. Mme Verdurin presents her guests at dinner like an auctioneer touting for a bid: 'Qu'est-ce que vous dîtes d'un savant comme cela?' she asks Forcheville, referring to Cottard who has just made a fatuous pun. 'Comment, vous ne connaissez pas le fameux Brichot? Il est célèbre dans toute l'Europe' is the 'blurb' with which she presents her tame scholar. The painter Biche (later revealed as Elstir) picks up the tone of the company, and utters daring inanities, thus winning an admiring comment from Forcheville. Even Mme Cottard, normally quiet, is tempted into a 'mot'. In this atmosphere of vanity and pretentiousness we see a brief exchange of glances between Odette and Forcheville. Forcheville insults the timid Saniette to such effect that the latter withdraws in tears, and Swann vividly recalls the look Odette gives Forcheville: 'elle avait brillanté ses prunelles d'un sourire sournois de félicitations pour l'audace qu'il avait eue, d'ironie pour celui qui en était victime; elle lui avait jeté un regard de complicité dans le mal' (I, 277). In that congratulatory smile we seem to see at once the vulgarity of Odette's soul, the beginnings of the liaison between Odette and Forcheville, and a culminating instance of the gross vanity and self-preoccupation that characterize the Verdurin salon.

In this context, we do well to remember a discussion of the symbolic value of the physical that occurs in the pages of *Combray*. It concerns the frescoes of Giotto, representing the Vices and Virtues. At first, Marcel does not care for these figures. Later, however, he comes to understand that the peculiar beauty of the frescoes lies in the large place accorded to symbols. The symbols are not understood or 'expressed' by the figures which represent them. Charity looks as if no charitable thought had ever entered her mind. She simply treads earthly treasures underfoot (as if trampling grapes) and passes her heart to God, like a cook passing a corkscrew up from the basement (I, 81). In the same way, the pregnant kitchen-maid at Combray, nicknamed 'La Charité', has no appearance of understanding the 'symbol' attached to her. Her swollen belly speaks for itself. She becomes, says Marcel, no less allegorical than the paintings, while they seem no less real than she. The symbol here refers not to an abstraction, or a thought, but to something much more literal and concrete. The physical action and gestures of Giotto's *Caritas* are charity not viewed as an abstraction, but observed in action and materially represented. The physical gesture or trait (like the swollen tongue of Giotto's *Envy*) is the point at which a particularity in an individual touches briefly, and unwittingly, on a universal pattern. This kind of non-abstract symbolization is one that Proust frequently employs.

He shows us for instance Legrandin, in the act of bowing to an important lady of the neighbourhood. He draws attention to a certain movement of Legrandin's fleshy rump and comments: 'je ne sais pourquoi cette ondulation de pure matière, ce flot tout charnel, sans expression de spiritualité . . . éveillèrent tout d'un coup dans mon esprit la possibilité d'un Legrandin tout différent de celui que nous connaissions' (I, 125). The material and physical here play the same role as in Giotto's frescoes. We could place Legrandin alongside the Vices and Virtues, under the heading: 'Le Snobisme'. The 'flot tout charnel' requires no conscious participation from Legrandin to reveal the vice operating through him.

By observing such points of contact between the physical and the moral world, Proust gives to the external world a moral significance, and the language of his moral concerns is usually specific and concrete. Its vocabulary includes such terms as 'the movement of Legrandin's rump', or 'Odette's smile'. Proust might well have said, along with Baudelaire: 'tout pour moi devient allégorie'. The allegory, however, is securely anchored in the observations of personal experience.[4] Proust plunges the reader into Marcel's subjective world. And the refusal to claim objectivity indicates in itself an awareness of limits and boundaries which are visible only to a detached and objective observer.

A metaphoric style

Proust then is concerned to create a whole world shaped and coloured by its having originated in the 'Ark' of Marcel's consciousness. In order to make accessible to the reader what is a personal and private world, Proust needs a very specialized style. One has only to think of the typically Proustian sentence, with its proposal of multiple subjects, images, comparisons and qualifications, to recognize that this is a style of unusual

[4] '. . . pour raisonneur qu'il soit, le narrateur n'exerce pas sa perspicacité sur une réalité dont d'autres que lui se porteraient garants, mais sur celle que ses sens lui ont révélée.' (G. Piroué, *Comment Lire Proust?* (Paris, Petite Bibliothèque Payot, 1955)).

density, which often combines rigorous analysis with a re-creation of the analogical movements of inward thought. Here, for instance, is a characteristically long sentence from *Un Amour de Swann*, where we penetrate into the inner workings of Swann's mind:

> Un jour que des réflexions de ce genre le ramenaient encore au souvenir du temps où on lui avait parlé Odette comme d'une femme entretenue, et où une fois de plus il s'amusait à opposer cette personnification étrange: la femme entretenue—chatoyant amalgame d'éléments inconnus et diaboliques, serti, comme une apparition de Gustave Moreau, de fleurs vénéneuses entrelacées à des joyaux précieux —et cette Odette sur le visage de qui il avait vu passer les mêmes sentiments de pitié pour un malheureux, de révolte contre une injustice, de gratitude pour un bien-fait, qu'il avait vu éprouver autrefois par sa propre mère, par ses amis, cette Odette dont les propos avaient si souvent trait aux choses qu'il connaissait le mieux lui-même, à ses collections, à sa chambre, à son vieux domestique, au banquier chez qui il avait ses titres, il se trouva que cette dernière image du banquier lui rappela qu'il aurait à y prendre de l'argent (I, 267)

As happens even more explicitly in the work of the contemporary novelist Nathalie Sarraute, a small phrase—'la femme entretenue'—acts here as the stimulus and centre of a number of associated or conflicting ideas. The phrase, once briefly used to describe Odette, recurs in Swann's mind, to evoke the sultry odalisques of Gustave Moreau, adorned with deadly flowers and precious gems. Swann defends himself against this image of Odette by evoking a benevolent and familiar Odette, made in the image of his mother and his friends. Proust's account of this defence not only describes it but ironically draws attention to the sham detachment and serenity with which Swann defends himself against a supposedly toothless but in fact mordant enemy: 'une fois de plus il *s'amusait* à opposer cette personnification . . .'. The benevolent Odette he has just fabricated is then associated with all the solid everyday details of his life— his collections, his room, his old servant. But here his mind betrays him as he adds his banker to the list. At once his mind moves back to its original preoccupation (now blanketed by comfortable images): the necessity of seeing his banker to arrange more money for Odette.

The sentence reproduces the rhythms of inner thought, moving, even while apparently pursuing quite another path, to an inexorable conclusion. Into the indecisiveness of the imperfect tense, the reiterated past historic makes a sharp intrusion, first with the ironic 'il se trouva',

then in the peremptory 'lui rappela'. Typically, the sentence brings
together images from life and from art; it combines diverse times and
fragments of diverse people and situations; typically too, it combines the
artful elaboration of a wish-image with the repressed but powerful
mechanisms of what Freud might call a 'censored' thought.

A careful look at the movement of almost any paragraph similarly
demonstrates how far we stand from the 'what happened next' style of
writing. We are, by means of style, to enter into a particular vision, but
our normal rather lazy reading habits are quite likely to get in the way.
Proust needs to dispel those habits and reawaken our sensitivity to the
nuances and complexities of language itself. We need to be attuned to a
kind of meditative reverie, in which we perceive not a single defined
thought, e.g. 'Swann rejects the notion of Odette as a kept woman and
simultaneously decides to see his banker to get more money for her', but
the multiple strands of image and emotion that create the shape and
colour of the thought. Analogy and metaphor, by the economy with
which they reveal shadowy emotional postures and significant associations of ideas and experience, are for Proust particularly useful tools.

But first we must be aware of the 'personality', the poetic value of
language: we must be sensitive to the fact that language has intimate
roots in personal experience. We all know something of the strange
fascination of certain words—words that have a special resonance for us.
Proust prevents our forgetting such oddities: he restores the magic, the
creative power of words. At the simplest level, he explores, for instance,
the evocative powers of names[5]—names with special associations, that
become a focus of the imagination. We see Marcel as a child going to
great lengths to bring the magical name 'Swann' into the conversation,
and thereafter trembling with guilty pleasure. Swann too works into his
conversations the name of the street where Odette lives, and even takes
to dining at a restaurant which happens to bear that name—La Pérouse.
The rue des Perchamps seems to the child as bizarre as its name—from
which, indeed, it seems to derive its 'personnalité revêche'. What first
attracts Marcel to the novel *François le Champi* is the sound of it.

The strange word 'Champi' he has never met before has no precise
meaning for him: it sounds mysteriously exotic and has, in his mind, a
'couleur empourprée'. The name 'Guermantes' acquires an orange
colouring from its final syllable 'mantes'. It is easy to see here a reflection

[5] In *Noms de Pays: le Nom*, there is an exquisite account of the pictures
which various place-names conjure up in Marcel's mind (I, 389).

of the preoccupations of the symbolist poets and of the Impressionists' emphasis on colour.[6] This correspondence of sound and colour[7] is also reminiscent of that wider interrelation of sense-impressions which Baudelaire expresses in the poem *Correspondances*, in which

Les parfums, les couleurs, et les sons se répondent . . .

and where physical properties are further linked with abstract qualities:

Il est des parfums frais comme des chairs d'enfants,
Doux comme les hautbois, verts comme les prairies,
Et d'autres, corrompus, riches, et triomphants.

A similar 'correspondence' of scents, sounds, colours, and moral qualities marks Proust's sensibility and style.[8] Just as names are forced to reveal their secret evocative powers, so sense-impressions reveal the secret inter-relationships of sound and sight, scent and emotion, colour and taste, in the 'ténébreuse et profonde unité' of the whole creation.

Sounds, for example, are often made both visible and tangible: 'des sons de la cloche de Saint-Hilaire . . . côtelés par la palpitation successive de toutes leurs lignes sonores, vibraient en rasant les fleurs, à nos pieds' (I, 170). Elsewhere they are translated into colour, moonlight, and an imaginary seascape, as when a passage from the Vinteuil sonata is transcribed as 'la mauve agitation des flots que charme et bémolise le clair de lune' (I, 208). Sound is expressed in terms of scent when we learn of the effect on Swann of the little phrase of the sonata, which 'lui avait ouvert

[6] In a perceptive article, 'Le Rôle des Couleurs dans l'Univers Proustien' (*Modern Language Review* LX, no. 2, April 1965), Dr Ninette Bailey shows how, in *La Recherche*, Proust adds colouration to the primarily graphic outlines given in *Jean Santeuil* and *Contre Sainte-Beuve*. She points out the mainly enriching and affective function of Proust's colours: 'Loin d'assurer une fidèle reproduction du monde de la perception, c'est à une transmutation du réel que travaillent les couleurs proustiennes' (p. 192).

[7] See also Roland Barthes, 'Proust et les Noms', in *Les Critiques de notre temps et Proust*, ed. J. Bersani.

[8] Links between Proust and Baudelaire are suggestively explored by Margaret Mein, *Proust's Challenge to Time* (Manchester University Press, 1962), especially Chapter V and Appendix I, and by Jean Pommier in *La Mystique de Marcel Proust* (Geneva, Droz, 1939; reprinted 1968).

plus largement l'âme, comme certaines odeurs de roses circulant dans l'air humide du soir' (I, 209), or when the phrase is briefly described as 'la phrase aérienne et odorante'. In the reverse direction, a visual impression is converted into sound when we see winter sunlight establishing itself on a balcony with 'un de ces crescendos continus comme ceux qui, en musique, à la fin d'une Ouverture, mènent une seule note jusqu'au fortissimo suprême' (I, 396).

Not only is one sense expressed in terms of another, but sense-impressions are also intimately linked with moral qualities or emotions. The smell of varnish on the stairs up which the child has to climb to bed concentrates his feelings of anguish and becomes 'plus toxique que la pénétration morale' (I, 28). Aunt Léonie's bedroom is saturated with 'mille odeurs qu'y dégagent les vertus, la sagesse, les habitudes, toute une vie secrète, invisible, surabondante et morale que l'atmosphère y tient en suspens' (I, 49). The scent of a roast chicken in the house at Combray seems the scent of one of Françoise's virtues.

Referring to the metaphysical poets, Eliot speaks of a 'mechanism of sensibility which could devour any kind of experience'. It is such a sensibility we find in Proust, one that interrelates physical sensations and moral perceptions. It is a sensibility that operates metaphorically, transferring the qualities of one thing to another, in such a way as to suggest the profound interrelationship of all experience. Objects, episodes or people meet in metaphorical connection, illuminating the common elements beneath diversity. Thus the pigeons in the Champs-Elysées briefly recall the lilacs of Combray when they become 'les lilas du règne des oiseaux' (I, 408), and a water-lily, caught in the cross-currents of the Vivonne, briefly illuminates the plight of 'certains neurasthéniques au nombre desquels mon grand-père comptait ma tante Léonie' (I, 169). A perfectly-roasted chicken, seen as a holy witness to the virtues of Françoise, acquires a priestly garb, with its skin 'brodée d'or comme une chasuble' (I, 122). Elements from the most diverse fields are brought together so that their metaphoric relationship instantly illuminates the frame of reference in which they are enclosed, and points to the way in which the individual mind assimilates experience and translates it into its own language of understanding.

The grotesque unnaturalness of Mme de Gallardon is seized and expressed by a transforming caricature, in which the posture of her head recalls 'la tête "rapportée" d'un faisan orgueilleux qu'on sert sur une table avec toutes ses plumes' (I, 329), while the closed windows of the

E

house where the Swanns live seem to the adolescent Marcel 'conscientes
d'être refermées, ressemblant beaucoup moins, entre la noble retombée
de leurs rideaux de mousseline, à n'importe quelles autres fenêtres
qu'aux regards de Gilberte' (I, 417). A window is likely to evoke other
windows: the association is determined by the general category 'window'
in terms of which we grasp the particularity. In Proust such rational and
obvious associations are, of course, frequent; others, however, like this
one, are determined by the analogies of personal vision, which isolate
and identify a certain internal vibration. The stimulus of that vibration
is linked not with other examples of the same class of objects, but with
other sources of the same vibration. The closed windows and Gilberte's
eyes come together to illuminate each other in their relation to the
consciousness of the narrator.

We need to remember that key-phrase in the experience of the *madeleine*: 'Chercher? pas seulement, créer.' The artist searches out the nature
of the internal vibration and creates an analogy which illuminates it.
The very disparity of the images pinpoints the unique nature of the
similarity. The windows and the eyes momentarily lose their ordinary
and functional characteristics, and our perception becomes an inner
perception, a response to the optical illusions of the heart. Our quiver of
inward recognition is aroused not by a picture of external reality but by
an artistic metamorphosis, representing Marcel's experience of those
long-lashed, self-conscious window-eyes, closed on an inaccessible and
mysterious world.

Art and life

It is not only personal experience that supplies the illuminating points
of reference. Swann and Marcel are both highly cultivated, and they
draw in consequence on all the resources of history, literature and art.
From the early pages of *Combray*, the plates decorated with motifs from
the *Arabian Nights* not only delight Marcel and Léonie, but cast a glow
of the wonderful on life about them. If the great-aunts had realized the
full extent of Swann's social life he would have seemed to them, we are
told, an Aristée, or even an Ali-Baba.[9] Léonie, avid for the daily gossip

[9] Jean Rousset draws attention to the association of Marcel with the
Arabian Nights: like Schéhérezade, he will save himself by the act of
creation. Swann, on the other hand, is linked with Saint-Simon and the

from Françoise, becomes a Persian prince, receiving 'la chronique quotidienne mais immémoriale de Combray' (I, 52).

Proust is concerned with the transformation of life into art, and in order to produce his alchemical change he uses a powerful admixture in art to the materials he is fusing—an admixture which serves to catalyse the transformation of the rest. He draws on the widely available elements of artistic tradition to enrich his vision, and at the same time to offer a world of experience common to Marcel and the reader, a world in which they may readily communicate. Mme de Guermantes in the church at Combray evokes a combination of Baudelaire, Wagner, and Carpaccio; Mme Swann's carriage is drawn by Constantin Guys horses; mistletoe berries in the Bois de Boulogne are round as the sun and moon in Michelangelo's *Creation* in the Sistine Chapel.

But the mingling of art with life is not a one-way process. If the face of Bloch gains by comparison with Bellini's *Mahomet*, the *Mahomet* also gains by its reflection in Bloch. If Swann's love-affair is changed by association with the Vinteuil Sonata, the Sonata is also changed into 'l'air national de leur amour'. Swann's association of Odette with Botticelli seems to justify his personal taste by an aesthetic sanctification, but Swann also understands that the painting he admires is itself the result of a reverse process, for the artists had, 'eux aussi, considéré avec plaisir, fait entrer dans leur œuvre, de tels visages qui donnent à celle-ci un singulier certificat de réalité et de vie, une saveur moderne . . .' (I, 223). The work of art, mingled in life, is not a static but an active and organic element, itself changing with new perceptions and circumstances, and changing the quality of life; for the world, Marcel later tells us, 'n'a pas été créé une fois, mais aussi souvent qu'un artiste original est survenu' (II, 327).

But Proust is aware that the intermixture of art and life is a double-edged sword. It may help us to understand life, or it may protect us from

---

social world. But at the end of the novel, Proust links both the *Arabian Nights* and Saint-Simon's *Mémoires* in Marcel's reflections on his own novel. He thus indicates the fusion of the two aspects of Marcel: Marcel-Swann, the socialite, and Marcel the artist who finally unites 'ces deux expériences antagonistes, l'expérience du miracle intérieur et l'expérience de la société, la magie et le mirage, la vérité et l'erreur, l'intemporel et le temps.' ('Problèmes de Structure' in *Entretiens sur Marcel Proust*, ed. G. Cattaui et P. Kolb, p. 200).

such understanding. Swann, who brings the sophisticated taste of the dilettante to all the aspects of his life, has chosen the latter course. He brings to the appreciation of his life something of the same pleasure he gets from reading Saint-Simon or the life of Lulli. He enjoys the process by which life aspires to art, but he remains a dilettante—an artistic consumer rather than a producer. From the insights which art affords him he creates nothing new, and his life runs to waste. It is left to Marcel to chronicle Swann's perceptions and thus create something new.

The most striking example of the mingling of art and life in *Du Côté de chez Swann* is undoubtedly that which takes place at the Saint-Euverte reception, where Swann's detachment from social life makes him see everything as a 'suite de tableaux'. His detachment has lent him an ironic distance. Instead of being absorbed by his social interests, Swann gazes at the entire scene with a dispassionate eye. Swann here views the world with what Professor Cocking calls 'a humorous sense of its contrast with a world of art which some of its features recall'.[10] But the irony moves beyond the immediate scene to the artistic model evoked, as when Swann contemplates a valet caught in the posture of 'ce guerrier purement décoratif qu'on voit dans les tableaux les plus tumultueux de Mantegna' (I, 324). The irony here pinpoints the arbitrary element in Mantegna's painting, in which a supernumerary warrior gazes with lofty indifference at the scene about him, in which St James is savagely martyred, or the Innocents slaughtered. And this vision of indifference reflects not only the lofty detachment of the valet but Swann's own detachment among the tumult of the social scene. Again, when Swann sees that the valet's hair 'a l'air à la fois d'un paquet d'algues, d'une nichée de colombes, d'un bandeau de jacinthes et d'une torsade de serpents' (I, 324), the description casts a comic light on what might also be seen in more heroic terms as 'the painter's triumphant mastery of all the rich and varied forms of nature'. There is an ironic disparity not only between the immediate scene and the artistic models Swann recalls, but between the artistic models themselves and the realities they purport to represent. Swann's irony casts doubt on the authenticity both of the social world he is viewing and of the world of art he recalls. Swann's mode here is that of sceptical wit, not of creation, and the result is not discovery but diversion. Rather than finding, as Marcel does, the intimate relations between the outer and the inner world, Swann preserves an ironic distance.

[10] J. M. Cocking, *Proust* (London, Bowes and Bowes, 1956), p. 30.

In his role of detached observer, Swann chooses to focus on a common superficial element among the guests—the monocle. He creates a series of sketches—the monocle of the observing novelist, the monocle which is the centre of gravity of the face of M. de Saint Candé, and the monocle which seems a symbolic fragment of M. de Palancy's aquarium. This last is linked with the figure of Injustice in the Giotto frescoes, so that the figures almost become allegorical portraits, linked by the motif of the monocle. Last in the monocle-series is 'un malheureux qui lui fit pitié' whom Swann, significantly, does not recognize. It is himself. And the narrator adds: 'Et sans doute, s'il s'était vu à ce moment-là, il eût ajouté à la collection de ceux qu'il avait distingués, le monocle qu'il déplaçait comme une pensée importune' (I, 347). But he does not see himself as part of the series—unlike Marcel, who, in *Le Temps retrouvé*, clearly recognizes himself among the 'dolls' of time at the Guermantes reception. It is only the Vinteuil sonata which shatters Swann's detachment and irony, brings him face to face with himself, and forces him to make discoveries. Thus Proust offers, through Swann, an example of a sterile dilettante view of art and the world. Proust makes it clear that for him life is not 'une suite de tableaux' for passive or ironic contemplation, but something demanding a constant and active response from the self.

The hawthorns

The passages describing the hawthorns at Combray vividly show how metaphors from many areas of experience may come together to create a new intensity. They are a sort of echo of the incident of the *madeleine*, and a foretaste of that reawakening of the narrator's sensibility which takes place in *Le Temps retrouvé* in response to other but similar stimuli.

We meet the hawthorns on the altar of the church, and first Marcel is fascinated by 'le geste de leur efflorescence'. He characteristically attempts inwardly to mime this 'gesture', in order to seize its character and find analogies within his experience which will correspond to the vivid gesture the immobile branches sketch in the air. It seems to him 'le mouvement de tête étourdi et rapide, au regard coquet, aux paupières diminuées, d'une blanche jeune fille, distraite et vive' (I, 112). Then, as he kneels before the altar, it is the scent that captures his attention and mingles with the colours to suggest new analogies:

Je sentis tout d'un coup, en me relevant, s'échapper des aubépines une odeur amère et douce d'amandes, et je remarquai alors sur les fleurs de petites places plus blondes sous lesquelles je me figurai que devait être cachée cette odeur, comme, sous les parties gratinées, le goût d'une frangipane ou, sous leurs tâches de rousseur, celui des joues de Mlle Vinteuil. Malgré la silencieuse immobilité des aubépines, cette inter-mittente odeur était comme le murmure de leur vie intense dont l'autel vibrait ainsi qu'une haie agreste visitée par de vivantes antennes, aux-quelles on pensait en voyant certaines étamines presque rousses qui semblaient avoir gardé la virulence printanière, le pouvoir irritant, d'insectes aujourd'hui métamorphosés en fleurs. (I, 113)

Almonds, frangipani, the freckled cheeks of Mlle Vinteuil, the buzzing of insects in spring-time hedgerows, all join together until the stamens acquire the vibrant vitality of 'insectes métamorphosés en fleurs'. By this drawing together of many diverse strands of experience, Proust achieves in prose the kind of intensity and unity normally associated with lyric poetry. Proust's vision, like the poet's, is active and organic: in it the parts of the world cohere in a new pattern.

The next time we meet the hawthorns is in the lane on the way to Tansonville. The previous vision, however, of the hawthorns exuberantly participating in the celebrations of the church, now joins with the present one, and transforms the hedge:

La haie formait comme une suite de *chapelles* qui disparaissaient sous la jonchée de leurs fleurs amoncelées *en reposoir*; au dessous d'elles, le soleil posait à terre un quadrillage de clarté, comme s'il venait de traverser *une verrière*; leur parfum s'étendait aussi onctueux, aussi délimité en sa forme que si j'eusse été devant *l'autel de la Vierge*, et les fleurs, ainsi parées, tenaient chacune d'un air distrait *son étincelant bouquet* d'étamines fines et rayonnantes *nervures de style flamboyant comme celles qui à l'église ajouraient la rampe du jubé ou les rameaux du vitrail* et qui s'épanouissaient en blanche chair de fraisier. (I, 138)[11]

The forms of the church shine out translucently through the forms of the hedge.

Now comes a struggle, like that recounted in the *madeleine* incident, a struggle to seize the secret essence which the hawthorns at once offer and conceal. But although the scent and the rhythms excite the child's mind tantalizingly, they keep their secret. Marcel leaves the hawthorns

[11] My italics.

temporarily, as he left the examination of the taste of the *madeleine*, then returns to try again: 'mais j'avais beau me faire un écran de mes mains pour n'avoir qu'elles sous les yeux, le sentiment qu'elles éveillaient en moi restait obscur et vague, cherchant en vain à se dégager, à venir adhérer à leurs fleurs' (I, 139). He will indeed learn, later in the novel, that it is not by exclusion and separation that he will find the reality he seeks. He learns from the painter Elstir that art and beauty are to be found everywhere, for they are within ourselves and not a monopoly of particular objects. As a result of this lesson, he tells us, he later learns to look at the sea, as he had not yet learned to look at the hawthorns, with inclusive and all-embracing eyes:

> Le long de la route, je ne faisais plus d'ailleurs un écran de mes mains comme dans ces jours où, concevant la nature comme animée d'une vie antérieure à l'apparition de l'homme . . . j'essayais de ne voir de la mer que la section où il n'y avait pas de bateau à vapeur, de façon à me la représenter comme immémoriale. (II, 902)

It is precisely the participation of the hawthorns in the rich context of Marcel's life that gives them their secret power, and not any separate and 'immemorial' identity.

After the contemplation of the white hawthorns, Marcel's grandfather calls the child's attention to a pink hawthorn, resplendent in 'une parure de fête' richer even than the ceremonial dress of the white hawthorn in the church. The pink hawthorn has a special prestige like that of the more expensive pink biscuits in Camus's shop, or of the cream cheese which, on special occasions, is made pink by being mixed with crushed strawberries. It belongs for the child to the world of special treats and Sunday-best . . . 'tout prêt pour le mois de Marie, dont il semblait faire partie déjà, tel brillait en souriant dans sa fraîche toilette rose l'arbuste catholique et délicieux' (I, 140).

While the young Marcel records his failure to capture the secrets of the hawthorns, this could only have been seen as a 'failure' by a writer who *did* know what is, in a sense, the 'secret' of the trees—the place and the meaning of the hawthorns in Marcel's life. They take their place in his weekday life of biscuits and treats, in the Sunday and spiritual life of the church, and in the inner life of the artist responding to his vocation. In the description of the hawthorn we see two processes at work: first, the illumination of the central 'frame' of the hawthorns by a sequence of diverse images (a girl tossing her head, the buzzing of insects, the freckles of Mlle Vinteuil, and so on) derived from Marcel's memories of other experiences, and secondly, the superimposition of two temporal frames, with the effect that we see the hawthorns at once as they were in the church and as they are in the lane. By what Proust calls elsewhere 'une répétition destinée à suggérer une vérité neuve' (I, 894), the frame acquires depth and intensity. As in that early process of colour photography, in which the colours, added one by one in layers, were then superimposed to create the desired polychromatic effect, Proust superimposes one element of experience on another to create the complex colouring of reality.

Just as diverse elements of experience combine to illuminate the hawthorn, so the hawthorn itself takes its place in another series—a series of mysterious appeals, promising a new reality. We have already observed that Marcel's reactions to the hawthorn recall his reactions to the taste of the *madeleine*. In *Un Amour de Swann*, the phrase from the Vinteuil sonata plays the same role for Swann, thus not only linking the *madeleine*, the hawthorn and the sonata, but causing a double vision of Swann and Marcel together. Swann's response to the sonata is illuminated by Marcel's to the *madeleine* and the hawthorn, and vice versa.

Superimposition of frames

The parallelism of Swann and Marcel is carefully developed. Marcel's jealousy of his mother is compared to Swann's jealousy of Odette: and just as Botticelli casts an aesthetic halo over Odette, so Bergotte casts a halo over Gilberte. Marcel's failure to salute his uncle Adolphe after the 'dame en rose' episode is echoed by Swann's refusal to salute Adolphe after Odette's accusations against him. The movements of Swann's infatuation with Odette are followed in those of Marcel's infatuation with Gilberte. Above all, the Sonata offers a view of Swann in a critical situation which reproduces a repeated crisis in Marcel's life—the moment when Swann fails, as Marcel, for a long time, will also fail, to respond to the appeal of art and beauty. The phrase briefly suggests the possibility of a renewal of Swann's soul; it announces to Swann 'la présence d'une de ces réalités invisibles auxquelles il avait cessé de croire' (I, 211). He feels 'le désir et presque la force de consacrer sa vie' (I, 211). The 'presque' in this sentence is crucial, for Swann's life thereafter pursues its mundane course. Yet, like the *madeleine*, and like the various stimuli Marcel encounters at the Guermantes reception at the end of the novel, the phrase reawakens for Swann moments of the past that had become inaccessible to his conscious memory. Swann recognizes the special quality of the Sonata, and realizes the extreme importance of his relationship with such impalpable but enduring things: 'la mort avec elles a quelque chose de moins amer, de moins inglorieux, peut-être de moins probable' (I, 350). But despite this realization, Swann does not find (as Marcel eventually will) the strength to dedicate his life to the pursuit of the reality and beauty he has glimpsed. By this parallelism of character, emotions and episodes, Marcel and Swann are made to reflect each other in such a way that each gains volume and significance from the other: in Marcel we feel the threat of Swann's failure, while in Swann we may see 'une sorte de "Marcel l'Ancien" qui fait les mêmes gestes sans leur donner la même signification que la grâce seule leur conférera.'[12]

This doubling of the two figures is characteristic of a Proustian method we may call the superimposition of frames, in which (as in the case of the hawthorns) scenes or episodes gain in density from a doubling of vision. We see two frames of vision operating simultaneously; Swann, for instance, among the splendours of the grand staircase at Mme de Saint-Euverte's, repeatedly sees in his mind's eye another staircase, adorned only by 'une boîte au lait vide sur un paillasson', but made irresistible by the presence of Odette. This vision is further multiplied by the projection into the décor of images from paintings which, at certain points, coincide with the scene Swann is viewing. Again, when Marcel describes the Allée des Acacias in the Bois de Boulogne, we see, moving in and out of each other, the frame of the child's vision of the Allée, the frame of the narrator's retrospective view, and the frame of the narrator's present view.

Sometimes the 'doubling' is achieved by a brief reference which brings together quite disparate episodes and shows their relationship. For instance, we see at Combray, through the eyes of the horrified Marcel, Françoise slaughtering a chicken with ferocious cries of 'Sale bête!' In *Un Amour de Swann*, we see Mme Verdurin, in the act of separating Swann from Odette, exclaiming vindictively: 'Non, mais voyez-vous, cette sale bête!' The reflection of the Combray scene gives body to this one, as the narrator shows us Mme Verdurin 'employant sans s'en rendre compte, et peut-être en obéissant au même besoin obscur de se justifier—

[12] Georges Cattaui, in *Entretiens sur Marcel Proust*, ed. G. Cattaui and P. Kolb, p. 210.

comme Françoise à Combray quand le poulet ne voulait pas mourir—les mots qu'arrachent les derniers sursauts d'un animal inoffensif qui agonise, au paysan qui est en train de l'écraser' (I, 285). We see Françoise elsewhere forming a shadowy backcloth to Marcel.[13] We see her, for instance, moved to tears by the description of the kitchen-maid's colic in a medical reference book, but totally callous to the maid in the flesh. Marcel perceives the same trait in himself when he finds himself unresponsive to Françoise's rather lofty notions of mourning: 'Je suis sûr que dans un livre—et en cela j'étais bien moi-même comme Françoise—cette conception du deuil m'eût été sympathique' (I, 154).

By this doubling of events, this exploration of recurrent patterns of behaviour, Proust offers his reflections on his experience in a language derived from, and still attached to, that experience. His reflections thus have not only intensity but precision. At the same time they offer the reader a poetic vision of life, in which new perceptions do not displace the old but qualify and enrich them. Proust takes, as it were, the magic-lantern slides of Marcel's life and multiplies them by the superimposition of other frames, giving them a further dimension—a thickness and solidity lacking in the flickering colours that shifted insubstantially about his room in Combray. Thus Proust creates a world of metaphor and metamorphosis whose effect is not, as in baroque poetry, to suggest the fickle inconstancy of changing forms, but to create out of inconstancy a fundamental unity, the identity of the self revealed in the enduring patterns of a unique vision.

Conclusion

Each part of this first volume ends, as we have seen, on a note of failure. The evocation of Combray returns to the 'tourbillon du réveil' (I, 187), Un Amour de Swann ends with Swann's acknowledgement of his mistake (I, 382). The third part ends with that haunting and plaintive reflection that 'les maisons, les routes, les avenues, sont fugitives, hélas, comme les années' (I, 427), recalling Baudelaire's similar complaint in Le Cygne:[14]

[13] See the interesting article by Jane Robertson, 'The Relationship between the hero and Françoise in A la Recherche du Temps perdu' (French Studies, October 1971).

[14] Jean Pommier draws the parallel in La Mystique de Marcel Proust, p. 21.

Le vieux Paris n'est plus (la forme d'une ville
Change plus vite, hélas! que le cœur d'un mortel).

The three failures recorded in the pages of *Du Côté de chez Swann* are a
prelude to further failures which the narrator records in the course of his
life. '*Le Temps Perdu*', Pierre Abraham comments, 'n'est pas l'ouvrage
d'un héros qui, rassuré sur lui-même et fixé sur sa vocation, s'exploite
comme une carrière de marbre pour en extraire des statues, c'est le
témoignage d'un homme qui poursuit anxieusement la route de sa
propre découverte et qui, sur cette route, se heurte à toutes les bornes,
glisse dans toutes les ornières, se perd à tous les carrefours'.[15] It is only in
Le Temps retrouvé that we move at last from the negative to the affirma-
tive mode—to the affirmation of an almost mystical faith in Art. Professor Pommier sums it up succinctly in these words: 'Ni le monde et ses
vanités, ni l'amour et ses détresses, n'introduisent dans la vie véritable.
L'Art seul en a la clef . . .'.[16] Reading the record of Marcel's successive
failures may be compared to hearing a once dumb man relating various
abortive efforts to restore his speech. It is a history not of despair but of
discovery, for the rich voice in which he tells of failure is a sufficient
testimony to the fact of eventual success. The three failures, by their
enduring existence in Proust's poetic and probing language, bear witness
to the novelist's ultimate triumph. Proust, through Marcel, has recaptured time lost, has discovered himself and, through art, has given body
to that 'vraie vie' he sought.

In the later volumes of the novel, each new incident and situation not
only is illuminated by the content of the first volume, but also casts a
retrospective light upon it, changing its lights and shadows. The child of
Combray moves through the glittering world in which Swann has preceded him. The world of Combray and pre-1914 Paris gives way to the
world of Balbec, of Doncières, and eventually of wartime and post-war
Paris. Figures already encountered in the first volume, even minor ones
like Norpois, or Cottard, or Bloch, reappear in different lights, and new
figures emerge, making new patterns. In the dance of relationships, begun
with Swann and Odette, Marcel and Gilberte, partners are changed, and
new couples (Marcel and Albertine, Saint-Loup and Rachel, Charles and
Morel) take the floor, complicating and diversifying the patterns.

[15] Pierre Abraham, *Proust, recherches sur la création intellectuelle* (Paris,
Les Editeurs Français Réunis, 1971), p. 128.
[16] Jean Pommier, *op. cit.*, p. 32.

Beyond the dance of the different couples, we see the formation-dancers of the social scene—the coteries and salons, which disperse and re-form, with new members and new styles. At the centre, giving unity to the brilliant social panorama, stands the observing consciousness of Marcel.

Like any great work, Proust's novel is not without flaws. A certain strain of self-indulgent preciosity makes itself felt at times, and there are occasional *longueurs*, where the prose meanders into rather murky abstraction and theorizing. Some readers may be dismayed at Marcel's obsessive introspection and egocentricity, though others may find this a small price to pay for the rich intensity of the world he uncovers. It is also arguable that Proust's guilt-ridden homosexuality affected, and even distorted, his view of life, particularly his view of human love, which he presents as an invariably one-sided affair. We may feel there is more generosity in the world than Proust usually allows, despite the glowing figures of Marcel's mother and grandmother. But Proust of course does not present Marcel as an impartial observer.

The novel may strike the reader as pessimistic in its stress on human egotism and folly, but its ultimate message is one that celebrates the beauty about us, and reaffirms the value of the individual human mind. There are times when even the most sanguine of us ask the Stendhalian question: 'N'est-ce que cela?' Are we but the sum of our dreams and disappointments? Marcel asks that question, and is appalled at the emptiness he finds within. Yet within the neurotic and apparently strerile Marcel lie the riches of a unique experience of life. We are all, Proust seems to say, 'récupérables'. The peasant Françoise is the poet of the *bœuf en daube*, and the Verdurins, for all their aggressive vulgarity, show disinterested kindness to Saniette. Cottard, for all his puns, is a brilliant diagnostician, and the pathetic old music-master of Combray conceals the great composer. Even the lesbian friend of Vinteuil's daughter will dedicate years of her life to piecing together the fragments of Vinteuil's uncompleted work. Proust explores a brittle and artificial social world, which is riddled with sexual deviations, sadism, and snobbery: the marvel is that it leaves us delighting in life's tragi-comic vivacity, and wondering at its riches.

Suggestions for Further Reading

A la Recherche du Temps perdu is best consulted in the three volumes of the *Pléiade* edition, edited by Pierre Clarac and Andre Ferré. (This revised text is also available in paperback, without the critical apparatus.) There is also a *Pléiade* edition of *Jean Santeuil*, with *Les Plaisirs et les Jours*, edited by Pierre Clarac and Y. Sandre. *Contre Sainte-Beuve* is available in the *Collection Idées* (Paris, Gallimard, 1954). The most generally useful volume of Proust's letters is *Choix de Lettres*, edited by P. Kolb (Paris, Plon, 1965). For other works, see the bibliographies suggested below.

The best biography of Proust, despite a tendency to overstress connections between life and literature, is George D. Painter's *Marcel Proust*, 2 volumes (London, Chatto and Windus, 1966, 1967). As it is impossible to deal here with the vast number of books and articles on Proust which are worth consulting, I refer the reader to the selected bibliographies in four recent helpful critical works: Germaine Brée, *The World of Marcel Proust* (London, Chatto and Windus, 1967); Adèle King, *Proust* (London, Oliver and Boyd, 1968); Jean-Yves Tadié, *Proust et le Roman* (Paris, Gallimard, 1971); and the invaluable collection of critical essays, *Les critiques de notre temps et Proust*, edited by Jacques Bersani (Paris, Garnier, 1971). A wide spectrum of critical opinion may also be conveniently found in *Proust, a collection of critical essays*, edited by R. Girard (New Jersey, Prentice-Hall, 1962), the *Yale French Studies* special issue on Proust (no. 34, June 1965), and the lavishly-illustrated *Marcel Proust, 1871–1922*, edited by Peter Quennell (London, Weidenfeld and Nicolson, 1971).